HANDKERCHIEF

Gracia Rich

Book Cover Design: Little Publishing LLC

Published By: Little Publishing LLC

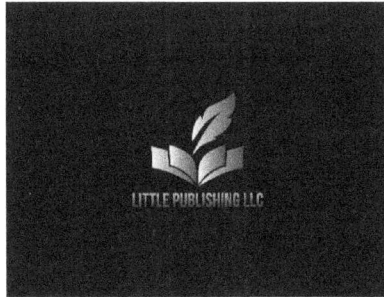

ISBN: : 978-1-7343314-3-1

Table of Contents

Prologue...1

One 3

Two 7

Three 15

Four..21

Five 27

Six..35

Seven 43

Eight 49

Nine 59

Ten..65

Eleven 71

Twelve 81

Thirteen..91

Fourteen 103

Fifteen...109

Sixteen 115

Seventeen...123

Eighteen..131

Nineteen..135

Twenty 141

Prologue

Tonight ends the way most of her nights do. Her party trail began at Club Coco around midnight, and from as far as she could tell, it had to be between 4 am and 5 am now. She's being pushed into a cab by Brent, at least that's what she thinks his name is. She wasn't paying much attention. Names were unimportant. He immediately slides in next to her. He's drunk, way more drunk than she's pretending to be. He's talking, but not making sense. His words are slurred, and he keeps attempting to push her dress up. She slides his hand away, not because she doesn't like his touch, but because she sees the cab driver looking into the rear-view mirror with hope, but he will not get a free show. Luckily, Brent's phone rings, and he answers, yelling into the receiver like a mad man. Who's calling him at this time of the morning? She thinks. Who cares? Is her next thought. Brent is a man she just met four hours ago. He offered to buy her a drink using the all too cliché line, "Another for me and the lady." She laughed, and he slid a bit closer to her at the bar. He's in advertising. "Ugh, everybody's in advertising," she thinks. Within an hour, they decide to continue their conversation at her apartment.

The cab stops in front of her building. Brent opens the door and steps aside to let her out. She studies the surrounding area. Where is the perfect place? He wraps his arms around her, and she giggles even though he hasn't said anything funny. He grabs her hand and tries to lead her to the door. She has other plans. She takes Brent's hand and leads him to the alley on the left side of the apartment complex. He doesn't object. His eyes lit up at the idea of doing something as risqué as sex in an alley. "Definitely from uptown," she thinks. As soon as they are deep enough in the darkness, Brent pushes her against the bricks and begins kissing her. She allows it. As he makes his way down her neck, he is breathing so loudly she fears someone may hear them. She wraps her arms around his neck, leaning closer into him. He squeezes her tightly, sliding his hand up her right thigh. His heart is beating so fast. It's like music. Being this close to him, she can feel his blood rushing. By this time, Brent has her dress up around her waist and his pants around his knees. She makes a slight sound when he enters her, just so that he knows she's still present. At least in body, her mind is elsewhere. Brent is now fucking her like an animal, almost knocking the wind out of her each time her back presses into the bricks. She doesn't like it, but she lets him continue. She wants him to enjoy it. He does. She's enjoying it too, just not in the same way. He finishes with a loud "Fuck" and let go of her legs. He turns his back to her and begins to right himself. He didn't even wait for me to finish. Selfish bastard, she thinks to herself. Again, he's talking. But it's just sound. She unsnaps her purse and places her hand on his shoulder. He places his hand on top of hers. His hand is warm. He leans into her. She reaches around with her right hand and, with no hesitation, cuts his throat with the serrated blade she took from her purse.

She hears him gurgle and pushes him forward. He turns around, staring directly at her, blood pouring around his hand as he's trying to keep it in. She gives him a smile and starts walking, not even waiting for him to fall. Brent wasn't a bad guy, he was actually pretty nice. He was just a casualty of war. A war he didn't know he was fighting. She glances back and sees him facedown as she turns the corner. She drops the knife back into her purse and hails a cab. A couple walks past and gives her a smile. She smiles back.

One

The funeral was quick and somber, as expected. James Chandler had many enemies and few friends. He had fucked over many people in his seventy years of living. He was a man who demanded respect. He had come from nothing. He built his company brick by brick with his blood, sweat and tears. He sacrificed the love of his family, and he was perfectly fine with that. James Chandler looked at people as assets and liabilities. When you could add to his wealth, you were worth keeping around. When you couldn't, you were better off dead. Jordan thought that he would have been dead a long time ago.

Jordan couldn't really say that she loved her father. She respected him, but she didn't love him. She had loved her mother. James provided her with a good life. She never wanted for anything, but maybe that was the problem. When she buried her mother five years ago, the pain was unbearable. She cried until she thought her eyes would bleed—not so with James. James was what she called him. Not father or daddy, but James. It was at his request. James Chandler wanted a son, and when he didn't get one, she was reduced to something he was responsible for. He loved his greyhounds more than he loved her.

Jordan had shaken so many hands that all the faces were now blending together. She was tired and just wanted it to be over. Her feet hurt, and her head felt as if someone was hitting her temples with a hammer. She didn't want to think about tomorrow. Tomorrow would be the day her life would change forever. She would now be the J in J. Chandler Enterprises. She felt the tears swelling in her eyes as she dabbed the corners to prevent her mascara from smearing. She wanted nothing more than to go home and get in bed. She wanted to forget everything—forget this funeral, forget James, forget her life. She had contemplated suicide numerous times, but she could never bring herself to do it. If only ending it all didn't have to be so painful. There was no way of doing it that would be simple, no falling off to sleep

3

and not waking up. Her tolerance for pain was low, at least for physical pain. She had mastered emotional pain long ago. It had been replaced by a numbness that could not be described. Nothing ever hurt anymore because she couldn't feel.

"Miss Jordan, Mrs. Beckett is here to see you," said Mildred, her father's maid. Mildred was a petite, stocky woman with gray hair pulled into a chignon. She had worked for James since Jordan was eleven years old. She was so young and full of life then. Funny how James had the ability to suck the life right out of people as he had done to Mildred. She looked even older than he did, even though she was seven years his junior. Jordan just nodded in agreement.

She hated Elizabeth Beckett. She was her father's longtime mistress. She had been a constant in Jordan's. Marcus Beckett, Elizabeth's husband, had been her father's business partner in the beginning stage of his business. Marcus found himself on the wrong side of an argument with James, and to pay for it, James began having an affair with his wife. Apparently, what Marcus did caused an irreparable rift because the affair never ended. Jordan remembered the last time she came creeping around like this. It was at her mother's funeral. Elizabeth feigned sadness, but Jordan could see the glee behind her eyes. She should have slapped her right across her powdered face, but she couldn't make a scene, and James would have made her pay afterward.

Jordan steadied herself. The sound of Elizabeth's heels crossing the foyer was making her blood boil. "Oh Jordie," she said, grabbing her into a fierce hug. With Elizabeth's long, red fingernails gripping into her back, she wanted to puke. She hated to be called Jordie. She was a grown-ass woman. She only allowed it because of James. That ended today. "I am so sorry about your father. He was a dear friend." Jordan felt the tears in her eyes turn to ice. Would anybody care if she knocked her out right now? She could blame it on her grief. She'd say she didn't remember it happening. She looked around the room as Elizabeth shed her crocodile tears. He would care, she thought, looking over at Marcus. He had learned about the affair a long time ago, but still, he remained. They had no children.

Jordan had heard that after a botched abortion of her father's child, old Lizzie had to have a hysterectomy. Poor Marcus never had a chance. Marcus was an attractive man. Jordan had a crush on him, but now he was like a silent shell sitting in his wheelchair staring into space.

"Thank you, Mrs. Beckett," she said, freeing herself from Elizabeth's arms. "I'm very happy that you and your husband were able to attend. James considered you both good friends." Jordan could taste that lie in her mouth. It was bitter as gall, and the lump it made in her throat hurt to swallow. "We had to come," said Elizabeth looking over her left shoulder at Marcus. "It was our duty to pay our respects. He was dear to us, and dear, I have always hated the way you called him James. After all, he was your father." Jordan clenched her fist.

"Would you had rather I called him Daddy, the way you did?" Elizabeth didn't flinch. She knew that Jordan knew about the affair. She was shocked that she hadn't told her mother but grateful that she had not. Elizabeth leaned in close to Jordan and said, "Keep your voice down, Jordie. What if poor Marcus hears? It would be the death of him." She then leaned back and smiled in a way that made Jordan's skin crawl. Her mouth painted red like some circus clown. Elizabeth didn't know that Marcus knew. Jordan gave her a fake smile.

"Thank you both again for coming," she said as she turned her back on Elizabeth and began to walk off. "Don't worry darling, you're not alone. We will see you next week at the reading of the will." Elizabeth smiled as she sauntered over to Marcus's chair. Jordan stopped in her tracks. The Will. Why would she be at the reading of the will? James wouldn't have. He couldn't have. Why would he publicly display his dirty laundry by leaving something to her in his will? Jordan bit her bottom lip. She knew why. It was his final stab at her, the last time he could publicly humiliate her. Even from the grave, she thought to herself. Touché James Chandler, touché.

Two

The wind was blowing through the sliding door of the patio, mixed with the coolness of rain from the thunderstorm. She remembered many nights standing on this very balcony looking out over the city. Tears began running down her cheeks. Why was she crying? From memories, definitely not out of remorse. David Jennings lay at her feet, a pool of blood collecting on his white cashmere rug. David loved white. He liked everything sterile. If he was watching his murder from somewhere, he was probably more upset about the stain than his actual death. His death had been untimely, but personal. Very personal. Not only had she spent times looking over the balcony, but she had also been hung across the railings many times.

She hurriedly scanned the room. She had to leave. She couldn't chance that someone would see her. She had been there longer than necessary. She didn't cry as she slid the razor across his cologne swathed neck. He never saw it coming, especially not from her. She was too meek, too good-natured. She had never fought back once when he slapped her, kicked her, put his fist into her ribs. She had taken it all. She waited patiently behind his bedroom door for him to return from his nightly coffee run. She moved the ottoman but an inch, and he tripped. She didn't have the strength to physically subdue him. But when he fell, she threw herself into her work. He panicked like she knew he would. She was certain he assumed she was a burglar that he could fight him off. But that was what she wanted him to think. She began attacking him like a wildcat, wielding the razor-like sharp claws. She furiously cut him across his face, his arms and his chest. The more he fought, the more excited she got. She probably would have let him off a little easier, but he kept fighting. He actually thought he could win. She laughed. She laughed loud and hysterically in the dark room, illuminated only by the moon. The knife went through his skin like he was made of butter. And the blood—warm, dark and rich—ran out so quickly like a deflated balloon. The contrast it made against the white in the room was like a beautiful, abstract painting. He should have known better. White catches everything, including his blood drained ass. He always did like it rough. She hoped this was rough enough.

For a moment, she felt something. She wasn't sure what it was. It wasn't guilt. She wasn't sorry for what she had done. Not in the least. In fact, she felt somewhat liberated. She was finally free of David. Sure, most people would have just left him, but that wouldn't have made it final. He would have come back, begging and trying everything he possibly could to get back into her good graces. She had no desire to watch him grovel. She wanted it to be done, with finality. And it was, this was final. She smiled as she glanced at the room one last time. David should have taken the hint. He might have still been alive if he had. She quickly removed her mask and stuffed it into her bag. She grabbed an oversized sweater she had left there some months back from the closet and put it on top of the black leotard. She placed her gloved hand on the doorknob and stepped outside into the hallway. The security camera was due to scan the doorway in the next twenty seconds. It only scanned the area twice an hour. She was never seen when she entered, but she would make sure she was seen this time.

"Five….four……three……two……..one," she counted as she reached the door from coming in the opposite direction in the hall. As soon as she put her key in the door, she heard the slight humming sound that the camera made. She knew she had been spotted. "Good," she thought to herself. She looked the same way she did so many times that she came to visit David. She was wearing a sweater over her leotard. On her way from dance class, no doubt. It was no secret to anyone who knew the two of them that she loved to dance. Her mother had put her in classes at five. It was actually one of the few things that she loved in this life. David's apartment was on the way from the dance studio, and she was known to stop in from time to time. She knew that Alan, the security guard, who was always positioned at the front desk, was at his lunch at this time. Therefore, if anyone was to ask him if he saw her enter the building, he would just say he was not at his post. Alan was the chatty type. He would more than likely go on to say, "Miss Jordan comes up here 'bout twice a week." He wouldn't be lying. She did have classes twice a week. Sometimes she would go, sometimes she wouldn't, but almost always she ended up here. It wasn't a stretch. She also knew that the security company in this building sent their film out to be reviewed and cataloged by ALIAS, and they were backlogged at the moment. She stored that fact into the back of her mind in case there was a problem. She turned her key and twisted the doorknob and began one of the biggest performances of her life. "DAVID," she screamed as soon as she turned on the light.

Grayson Jeffcoat had been a cop for ten years. He didn't hate it, but he definitely didn't love it either. It just seemed like a natural progression after the army. He liked the structure of law enforcement, but he was tired of violence, of the bodies. He had seen enough bodies. War will do that to you. He had to admit that sounded stupid, even in his own mind. What type of cop hopes to never see a dead body? Only a very lucky one and he had never been that lucky.

He looked over at Vicki's desk. Her he didn't get. Victoria or Vicki, as she insisted he call her, was a beautiful woman. But she was also one of the toughest cops he had ever seen. She'd been on the force was twelve years and had been shot twice. Once on a robbery gone wrong and another by a drug addict fleeing a crack house. She'd been his partner since he joined the force. Fortunately, neither of them had been shot again. Now shot at was another story.

"My boyfriend is dead. He's dead. She shouted into the phone to the 911 operator. "Miss, you need to calm down," said the operator. "Are you sure he's dead?" "He's bleeding out all over the rug. His throat is cut. Oh my god, oh my god," she shouted to the operator between sobs. "Ma'am, we are sending someone to your location right now. They will be there shortly." she continued crying into her phone until she pressed end. She looked over at David. She felt a grin spill onto her face. It wasn't nice to laugh. It wasn't polite, but it was fitting. David had always threatened to kill her. She had always felt that one day he would get mad enough to do it. That would be so stereotypical. Young, rich socialite killed by obsessive boyfriend. The tabloids wouldn't be able to get enough. If James were alive when it happened, he would have no doubt bought all of them only to put them out of business. Not because he cared about her, but because of the mark it would leave on his name. He would never have that. Before it was all over, she would have been made some sort of heroine in a robbery gone wrong, or something like that.

David was turning that horrible greenish-blue color. She was sure that he was stiff as a board, but she wouldn't touch him. That was too morbid. She kept her distance behind the bar that wrapped around to the kitchen. She was careful not to touch anything more than necessary. She was certain that it wasn't going to be a big deal with them finding her fingerprints there. Hell, she practically lived there, but she didn't need them in places that would garner suspicion. That was anywhere near David right at this moment.

She suddenly heard footsteps coming down the hall. She crouched down beside the door and did her best scared impression. "Ma'am, are you there," she heard a voice ask. "Open up, it's the police." She reached up and slowly turned the doorknob without getting out of her position. As soon as the door was cracked, officers moved into the apartment. One of them went over and touched David. "He's dead," he said, looking over his shoulder to the officer standing at the left of her. "Call the coroner and get Jeffcoat down here." The officer nodded and moved out into the hallway and began talking on his cell.

"Ma'am, are you ok?" "Do you know the victim?" She didn't answer. She knew how to pretend to be in shock. The officer walked over and offered her his hand so that she could get up from the floor. She took it and slowly rose from her position by the door. "Ma'am, how did you get here? Do you live here?" he asked her again. "No," she answered slowly. "This is my fiancé's apartment." "Where is your fiancé? Is he here?" "He's over there," she pointed slowly at David's body, still lying on the floor. "His name is David James Anderson, and he's dead." She crumbled to the floor and began sobbing uncontrollably.

The officer stepped out into the hallway, where his partner was finishing his conversation. "Is the coroner on the way? We need to get this body out of here. How about Jeffcoat? She's hysterical. Someone needs to get here quick. You know I'm not good with this type of stuff. So much for doing Bradley a favor, I could have been in bed right now. Or at Angie's." They both laughed. "The coroner is on his way. Jeffcoat should be here any minute. He was already in the area." "Great," he replied. "I wonder what he is going to make of this. At that time, they spotted the coroner coming up from the stairwell. "He's in there," the cop stated. The coroner just nodded and went through the open door. The older cop followed behind him.

The younger cop stopped at the doorway and looked at her. "Ma'am, do you need anything? Would you like a cup of water?" She gave no reply. She just continued staring at the wall farthest from her. It, too, was white like everything else in the room—stark and plain, yet revealing and unflawed. She understood David's taste. Maybe in a few days, she would buy this complex. It would be a perfect little memento for what she had done. She would never live here, of course. She would never be caught on that side of town if it wasn't for the fact that she had fallen in love with the wrong man. He was wrong from the very beginning. She knew it, but she was drawn to him. She always had that bad boy thing in her. He seemed fun and exciting in the beginning, but that all changed. David was a son of a bitch and deserved what he got. Her only thought was that she wished it had happened sooner.

"Miss," she felt a hand on her shoulder. She turned, expecting to see the cop that was just speaking with her. She didn't find him there. What she did find pleasantly surprised her. "Miss," he stated again. "My name is Grayson Jeffcoat. I'm the lead investigator from Homicide. May I ask who you are?" She just looked at him. She was stunned. She wasn't sure if it was because he asked who she was as if he was not familiar at all, or if it was because he was fine as hell. Grayson Jeffcoat stood around six feet four with broad shoulders, muscles everywhere. She could tell by the way his buttons seemed to strain against the fabric of his dress shirt. He had short black hair, blue eyes, and a jawline that could cut glass.

"Miss, do you need a moment?" His voice snapped Jordan out of her dream world. At that minute, she was not even aware that he was speaking

11

to her.

"Do you know the deceased?"

"Yes," she replied. "He was my fiancé."

"And your name is?" Jeffcoat asked. She looked warily at him, her brown eyes glowing like honey. "My name is Jordan Chandler." "Ok," he said, jotting that down in a notepad he held in his hand. "Ms. Chandler, do you live here."

"No," she replied. "I just come by occasionally when I finish dance class." Grayson gave her a once over and noticed she was wearing something indicative of that. He noted that as well. "I was told that you found him," he said. "Yes, he was there on the floor when I arrived." "Did you notice anything out of place? Was the door open? Did you see anyone strange hanging around?" She looked at him as if he were crazy. She had heard before that this was the way these things seem to work, but she was really getting bored with all these questions. "I didn't see anyone. The door was locked. I used my key to open it. I haven't looked around to know if anything is out of place. I didn't move around a lot. I saw David there, and I screamed..........I called 911. But it was too late, oh god, it was too late." And with that, she started crying again.

Grayson gently put his hand on her shoulder and led her into the hallway. He quickly darted back inside the apartment and grabbed a chair from the dining room table. He placed it against the wall and motioned for Jordan to sit down. "I know this is hard for you, Ms. Chandler. I will see if I can get them to move a little faster so that we can get out of your hair. This has been a terrible experience for you. I know that you never expected to find this." Jordan began to cry even harder. Grayson reached into his trench pocket and offered her his handkerchief. "No, thank you," replied Jordan. "I have one." She reached down into her bag and pulled out a white lace handkerchief and began wiping her eyes with it. Grayson turned his back to her slightly and gave her a second to compose herself.

"I would like to leave now," she said, standing. "I need to go home." Grayson turned around at the sound of her voice. "I understand," he said.

12

"But I will have more questions for you. Would you be willing to come down to the police station tomorrow morning?" Jordan just stared at him. She really didn't feel like going to the police station in light of everything that had happened in the last couple of days. "That won't be possible," she said. "They are reading my father's will tomorrow morning, and I won't be available until later." "I'm sorry to hear about your father," he said. "This has really been a rough time for you, hasn't it?" Jordan made no reply. "This is my card," he said, reaching into his pocket. "Call me when you are available to talk. I can come by your home or office if need be. Jordan took the card from his hand and dropped it into her bag. "I will give you a call." She began walking towards the elevator.

"Ms. Chandler," he called out to her. "This needs to be done sooner than later. Please make time. Do you need a lift home? I can have one of my men escort you." "No, thank you," she replied. "I will be fine, and Investigator Jeffcoat, I will make time very soon for your questions." Grayson gave a glance in her direction and headed back into David's apartment.

Jordan smiled as soon as the elevator doors closed. She reached into her bag and pulled out Grayson's card. So, Investigator Jeffcoat, you plan to question me. She thought to herself. That could be very interesting indeed. How would she play it? The saddened fiancée, the abused girlfriend, or upper-class bitch who really doesn't give a shit. She could throw some names out there to give misdirection so that they could never find out who actually killed him. Hmmmmm, all of those are interesting choices. As she reached the ground floor, she decided that she wouldn't decide just yet. Whichever one turned on when she decided to see him, that was the one she would play. It would be a surprise, even to her. She walked to her black Audi parked in the back of the parking garage and drove home. Her back hurt from all that tussling with David. A hot bubble bath was in order. That and a bottle of vodka. She thought back on the handsome Grayson Jeffcoat. Damn, he's sexy. Maybe if he gets too close, I can do a little damage control. Controlling men with pussy is far easier than any blackmail scheme or hit around, plus it's much more effective. She smiled to herself as she turned onto the interstate.

Three

When Grayson turned the corner the next morning to enter the station parking lot, he wasn't prepared for what he saw. Reporters. Reporters were everywhere. They were actually mobbing the police station. As soon as he got out of the truck, he was approached by two of them. "Are you Grayson Jeffcoat," one of them asked. "Are you thinking she's somehow involved? Someone said that you told her there would be more questions," said another. Grayson was not a fan of the media. He had learned a long time ago that you can't say anything to them. They twist everything. He even opted out of saying, "no comment." He kept his head down and burrowed his way through them to the entrance of the station, hurrying in and shutting the doors firmly behind him.

"Why the circus?" he asked when he reached his desk near the middle of the station. "Are you serious?" replied Vicki. "She is all they've been talking about."

"She who?" he asked. "Jordan Chandler, you idiot," she said. "Weren't you there last night?" "There where? I was at a murder scene, not a social event," he responded. "They are acting as if the president is here, or better yet, Brad and Angelina." He got a few laughs from some officers at their desks on that one. "They want to know about her," continued Vicki. "How is she tied to the murder?" "Ok, Victoria, explain to me what you're talking about."

"Gray, Jordan Chandler is who I'm talking about. She is the daughter of James Chandler of J. Chandler Enterprises. Hell, the company is probably hers now that the old bastard has died. She is worth billions. That's why everyone is up in arms about this shit. Oh, I'm sorry. This unfortunate murder. Who was the poor soul anyway?

Grayson finally sat down in his chair. "So, you mean to tell me that the girl I saw last night, curly hair, big, brown eyes, wearing a sweater and some sort of dance thingy is worth billions?" "That's about it," said Vicki. "So, tell me, what was she doing there?" "I'm not exactly certain," said Grayson. "She said this guy was her fiancé. That kind of makes me wonder since you said she's worth billions. She said she stops by there from time to time when she is coming from the dance studio. I didn't have time to corroborate her story, but she did have a key to the place. She seemed really broken up about it." "Seemed," asked Vicki. "What are you getting at, Gray?" "Well, she did a lot of crying. I was told by the officers at the scene that she seemed to be in shock when they arrived. She was glued to a position by the door. She didn't talk much. She never went close to the body, almost like she was afraid to. When the guys were in with the coroner preparing to take the body back to the morgue, she never asked to go with them. She actually told me she needed to go. It just seemed kind of weird for someone who finds the person they were willing to spend their entire life with lying in a pool of blood. And then there were her eyes."

"Ah, here we go with you and these hunches," said Victoria. "What was wrong with the girl's eyes?" "Nothing, and that's the problem. She was crying, but there was no redness to her eyes—not one hint. It was just like turning on a faucet and the water spilling out. She looked sad, but there was no real feeling there," he said. "Well, you know how rich people are. It's all about image. I'm sure she's been taught to cry without making a scene. And who knows, maybe she felt if she didn't cry it would breed some sort of suspicion. Even though she didn't know that with you, everything breeds suspicion." They both laughed.

"Vicki, his name was David James Anderson. See what you can find out about him for me. I think I'm going to pay a visit to Ms. Chandler and see how broken up she really is over her former future husband." "I'll get right on it, and Gray..," she said. "Be careful. When people go snooping in things that powerful people don't want found out, bad things tend to happen." "Don't worry, Victoria. I'll be fine." He grabbed his jacket.

"How's the Chief holding up," Grayson asked, pointing to the closed door across the room. "Oh, he's fine. He was out here earlier, huffing and puffing at reporters. He actually scared off a few of the younger ones. The veterans like Horace and Jacobs, however, only find him amusing. They will probably be out there all day hoping for a glimpse of her or a story from you." "Well, I wish them luck with that," Grayson said sarcastically as he headed for the side lobby. He would go through to the adjoining fire department and go out on their backside. That way, he could avoid all reporters hoping to get something out of him.

Jordan woke up with a sense of dread. She knew that today would be a day that she would never forget. Aside from James's funeral, this had to be the most difficult day she'd have to endure. Not because she was so concerned about what was left in the will, more so because of who was going to be there. She felt her stomach turn at the thought of Elizabeth Beckett smiling back at her from the other end of the table. "That bitch." She really wanted to claw her eyes out, but James had made sure that wouldn't happen. She couldn't touch her now. It would be impossible since she had a stake in the company now. Jordan pulled herself out of bed and headed for the shower. There was no need to attempt to put off the inevitable.

"Thank you all for coming," said William Allington. Mr. Allington had been James Chandler's lawyer for as long as Jordan could remember. He and her father had been lifelong friends, and she was certain that if there was one person alive who was privy to all of her father's secrets, it was him. She looked around the room at the motley crew before her. There was Elizabeth and Marcus Beckett, Mildred, her father's longtime maid, Mr. Allington and one lone man sitting in the back corner of the conference room. She had never seen him before and had no idea what his purpose was. "I feel somewhat saddened for our purpose here today," began Mr. Allington. "James was a dear friend of mine. We have had many good times in this life, probably more than should be allowed any man. His passing has pained me deeply." Jordan let out a sigh. Maybe he was pained. She wouldn't bet on it, though. James had a way of turning a friend into an enemy or even worse, making a friend beholden to him, forcing him to do his bidding. With Allington, it could have gone either way.

Jordan looked over at Elizabeth Beckett. She looked like the cat who

17

swallowed the canary. Jordan didn't like that look. She knew something. She wasn't sure what Lizzie knew, but her face showed her that something was up. She smiled at Jordan. Not a genuine one, but one of those fake, pinched face smiles. Jordan hated her. If hate was the strongest word she could use. She despised her. Marcus sat beside her in his wheelchair. He had a sympathetic look in his eyes as he looked down the long, mahogany table at her. She knew that Marcus was truly her father's friend. He forgave him even after he knew that he was fucking his wife. He took the high road. She admired that about him. He didn't deserve the bitch he was married to. She was trash. She had wanted him to leave her so many times, toss her out on her ass. But she had found out long ago that Elizabeth controlled everything now, and even if Marcus had saved up a little something for himself, where would he go now. For as much as she liked Marcus, Jordan sometimes wished he would die. At least he would be at peace and free of her. She didn't love him. She paraded her many lovers right in front of him as if daring him to do something. She felt her stomach clench. "Lizzie," as Marcus called her, made her want to puke. She really wanted to get this over with. Whatever James had planned on doing needed to be done, and quickly.

Allington went on with his mini eulogy before really getting down to the brass tacks. "I, James Chandler, being of sound mind and body hereby leave fifty-one percent of my company to my daughter and sole heir, Jordan Chandler. Jordan will retain my current title of CEO, all decisions regarding the company will come through her. She must approve everything. The remaining forty-nine percent I leave to my longtime friend, Marcus Beckett and his wife, Elizabeth. Marcus will be the CFO of the company. Jordan felt her fingertips tingle. Her head felt as if she was going to pass out. How could he? How could he make her an almost equal partner? Sure, he named Marcus, but everyone knew that Elizabeth pulled the strings. Now she had a say in her life, her money, her future. That was not going to do. Not at all.

Jordan found herself in a daze until she heard the click of Allington's briefcase. She had no idea what else he said. Her mind was too busy racing on what to do about Elizabeth Beckett. She watched as Mildred came down

18

to her end of the table. "Miss Jordan, your father wasn't so bad, after all. He left me a nice little nest egg to retire on. I will finally get that vacation I wanted." She seemed thrilled. Jordan clasped the woman's hands and gave them a little pat on the top. "I'm happy for you, Mildred," she said. "You deserve it. You were very good to my father despite the fact he wasn't the same to you." Mildred nodded and left the room. Elizabeth had joined her at the head of the table, with Marcus rolling behind her.

"Oh Jordie, looks like we're partners. That's just like James, wanting to take care of everyone. What a dear man," Elizabeth said, giving her one of those hugs she loathed.

"We will always have your best interest at heart," said Marcus as he shook Jordan's hand. She believed him. He wouldn't do anything to hurt her, but he could only do what he was allowed. She was certain that as soon as his eyes were closed, be it in sleep or death, Elizabeth would do her best to ruin her or at least put her in the poor house.

"We will discuss the details later this week, dear," Elizabeth said, stroking the faux fur stole she wore around her neck. "Marcus and I have other engagements to attend to." "Come on, Marcus, we are due at Baxter's in an hour," she said as she headed for the door. "It will all be okay, Jordan. Don't worry, I'll make sure of it," said Marcus with a smile as he wheeled behind his detestable wife.

Jordan dropped back down into her chair. Mr. Allington joined her at the end of the table, along with the strange man from the corner. "Don't worry so much, Jordan," Allington said. "Marcus is an excellent businessman. You are lucky to have him."

"It's not Marcus that concerns me," she said, looking at him with a grimace. "Ah, well, I understand. But just so you know, if Marcus dies, Elizabeth will own his share. If you outlive them both, the company is solely yours. Your father made sure of that." Jordan made a mental note of that. That was the best news she had gotten all day.

"Jordan, this is Gregory, my son," he said, gesturing towards the younger man who had joined them at the end of the table. Gregory was tall and slender like his father. He had brown hair and eyes. "Greg is going to be taking over my firm. He is a competent attorney in his own right, and I'm just getting too old for this. Your father's estate was the last of my retainers. I'm done with this. Greg is up to par on everything and is now your corporate attorney, please consider him for your personal matters as well."

"It would give me great pleasure to work for you, Ms. Chandler," Greg said, grabbing her hand. Too eager, she thought. He didn't even wait for her to extend her hand first. She shook his hand. His grip was light. She felt her face tighten just a little and feared that Allington had noticed. He hadn't. He was beaming over his son, as a parent should. A good one anyway. "I look forward to working with you, Greg," she said sweetly as she let go of his hand. The elder Allington smiled.

"Well, that wraps things up here. I will send the remaining paperwork to your office later this week for your signature." "That will be fine," she replied. "Thank you, Mr. Allington, for putting up with James all these years." He gave her a hug. "Thank you, Jordan. I know that your father never said it to you, but he was proud of you. You were all he had left of your mother, and he loved you both. He told me so many times. Men like James just never knew how to express themselves. I'm sorry for your pain," he said. Jordan nodded in agreement as the Allingtons left the conference room. She really didn't know what to say. She understood what the old man was trying to do, but it didn't matter. She hated James Chandler. The grave was the best place for him.

Four

The taxi pulled up to the twenty-one-story building that was J. Chandler Enterprises. Grayson Jeffcoat stepped out onto the busy street. He had left his truck behind at the police station in his attempt to sidestep the reporters. The building itself was intimidating, all mirrored windows and shining silver steel. It looked very odd in the middle of the industrial side of town. All of the buildings there were much older and paled in comparison to the gleaming, towering obelisk.

Grayson threw the remainder of his apple in the trash. He had grabbed it off his desk since a real breakfast hadn't been available this morning. When he walked in through the sliding glass doors, there was a large black desk with a man with blonde hair sitting in a swivel chair. His name tag said Steven Wingate.

"Good morning, Mr. Wingate. I'd like to see Ms. Jordan Chandler. Is she available?'. The blonde began smiling. "Well, mornin' yourself," he said with a Southern drawl. "And you can call me Steve. Everybody does." Grayson smiled back. "Well, Steve," he started. "Is she available?" "Do you have an appointment," Steve asked. "You do know you need an appointment to see her, right? And what is your name? You never said." "It's Grayson."

"Grayson.....well, I do like that name. I don't see you on the list. What is your business with Ms. Chandler," Steve asked, now leaning over the desk a little. "I love your boots, Grayson," he said, smiling. Grayson laughed, his face turning a bit red from Steve's attention. "Thanks, Steve. Do you think I can see her?" Grayson flashed his most dashing smile. "Well, let me see, said Steve forgetting all about what Grayson's nature of business was. "I tell you what, I'm going to call up to her assistant, Rebecca, and see if she can squeeze you in. Please have a seat over there." He watched as the man picked up the receiver and pressed a button. He knew he was wrong for encouraging Steve, but it was much easier to have him do it as a favor than to let him know he was a cop and alert everyone in the building.

"Rebecca, hey, Steve here. Is Jordan available?" Grayson could not hear the voice on the other end as Steve turned his back at the counter. "Because she has someone waiting to see her, and he is gorgeous. GORGEOUS," said Steve. "Ok, wait, your gorgeous or my gorgeous," Rebecca asked curiously. "Everybody with eyes gorgeous," he replied. "Is he single," she asked. "No ring, honey," he replied. "Is he straight," she asked. "Undecided, but I hope the hell not," Steve replied. Grayson had to mask his laugh with a cough. This conversation was about him, and they were having it as if he wasn't even in the room. "Well, I'll never see him if I don't allow him to come up," she said. "Tell him I have a window of about twenty minutes if he comes up now. And he better not disappoint." "Trust me, honey, it's the stuff that dreams are made of. See you at lunch," Steve said, hanging up the phone.

"Ok, handsome, she can see you. But you have to go up now. Penthouse suite," said Steve. "Thanks a lot, Steve," Grayson replied. "Can I ask you something personal," Steve said. Grayson had an idea where this was going, but he had gotten him in, so he would allow him one question. "Sure, go for it," Grayson replied. "Are you one of Ms. Jordan's suitors?" Grayson laughed. "No, my visit is totally business." Steve's smile widened. "So, what are you doing later," Steve asked. "Only one question, remember," Grayson replied as he walked around Steve's desk. "I get it. Playing hard to get," said Steve. "I like it." Grayson laughed as the elevator closed.

When the sliding doors opened to the Penthouse office, Grayson was met by another black desk. This time a woman was sitting behind it. She had long, red hair. She just stared at him, not saying anything. "Hi, I'm Grayson Jeffcoat. I'm here to see Ms. Chandler." She still said nothing. "Miss," he said, placing his hands on top of her desk. "Sorry," she said, snapping out of her trance. "I'll let her know you are here to see her. I'm sorry, but you said your name was what again," asked Rebecca. "It's Grayson. Grayson Jeffcoat," he replied. "Right, right," she repeated, walking towards the door to her left. She made a note to buy Steve lunch. He was everything he said he was.

Rebecca stepped inside the office. "Jordan, there is a Mr. Grayson Jeffcoat here to see you." Jordan looked up from the computer screen. She knew that name, but she couldn't quite place it. Today had been one of those days. "Did he say what he wanted," she asked Rebecca. "No," she said, smiling. "Why are you smiling like that," asked Jordan. She was already irritated, and she didn't have time for whatever game Rebecca was playing. "No, Jordan. I don't know why he's here. She caught the message that Jordan was sending and stepped back into the doorway. Apparently, Jordan wasn't in the mood. Jordan stood behind her desk and thought. His face seemed to materialize. *That Grayson Jeffcoat. The fucking nerve. How dare he show up at her office without an appointment?* Maybe he had figured something out and was hoping to catch her off guard. She doubted it. He didn't seem like he was that smart. "Are you sure he didn't say why he was here," she asked Rebecca. "No. Not to Steve or me. He just said he needed to see you." "Okay, please show him in," Jordan said, smoothing down an errant curl. Rebecca returned to the waiting area. "Ms. Chandler will see you now. If you would please follow me." Grayson rose to his feet and followed the redhead to Jordan's office door.

"Good morning, Mr. Jeffcoat," she said as Rebecca closed the door. "I didn't expect to see you so soon." "I wasn't planning on making this trip so soon, either. That was before I got to work and was mobbed by reporters who were interested in your involvement with my murder investigation."

"Reporters, you say," she asked, walking from around the desk. "They go crazy over any tidbit they can get. By the way, Investigator Jeffcoat, you never said how they found out I was there." Caught off guard, Grayson thought about that for the first time. How did they know? No one took any pictures of her, and she didn't leave through the front entrance of the building. That meant that one of his people gave the tip and for an undisclosed amount of cash, no doubt. He would handle that when he got back to the station. "I'm working on finding the leak as we speak," he said, trying not to give himself away. "I see," she replied.

"So, you own this company?" "My father owned this company. He died, and now I own it," she replied. "You look different from the other night. I would have never guessed that this is where you hang your hat," he said. "Also, you can call me Grayson."

Jordan continued to walk around the room as Grayson watched her. "Investigator Jeffcoat," she started. "It's Gray….." She lifted her finger to her lips. "Please, if you would let me finish. This is what I deduce. You don't know who your leak is. You didn't even think about that before you came running over here to grill me with your questions. I feel that you need to figure out how information is leaving your department before you continue your assault on me." Grayson just stared at her as she continued with her tirade. "Assault," he asked. "I haven't asked the first question yet." She moved closer to the window behind the desk. He was staring at her. She didn't like that. He had a calm look about him. She didn't care for that too much either. She figured that most cops would get upset if someone confronted them with what they were doing wrong. He didn't. He just gave her a matter-of-fact look that made her want to scream. She would have sworn that she almost saw a smile creeping into the corner of his mouth. "And I would never call you Grayson. That implies that I would wish to associate with you outside of this terrible business, which, believe me, I do not," she finished her statement striking her fist into her palm for emphasis. Grayson got up from his chair to stand in front of her desk.

"I see you've had a terrible day. Maybe tomorrow would be much better." She narrowed her eyes at him. He steadied himself because she looked as though she was itching to cut him with the very next word out of her mouth.

"Tomorrow won't be any better," she replied. "Well, it will have to do."

"There are questions that need to be answered. A man is dead. A man you claim to be your fiancé." Jordan slowly slid into her chair. She had to get herself together. Her brief performance had caused uneasiness in the room. It was obvious that Investigator Jeffcoat had gotten a read on her. She wondered which read was it. Did her uncaring façade lead him to believe that she was not as in love with her fiancé as he would have thought, or did he know that she was playing some kind of game? She had to figure it out fast.

"Ms. Jordan," Grayson started. 'I understand that you have been through some traumatic events in the last few days. I mean with your father dying and then someone killing the man you loved. I would be upset too. It's easy to lash out at the world when you're hurting. I get that, but I will be back tomorrow for some answers. Mr. Anderson's family deserves answers and justice. We can't get either if you don't cooperate."

"Family," she asked. "David didn't have any family." "He did," he replied. "His brother, Tom, came down and officially identified the body. He and David had been on the outs for some time. But he was still his brother. It was a sad reunion, to say the least." Jordan felt a little flip in the bottom of her stomach. David had told her that he was an orphan, abandoned by his family. She had believed that. She had never asked any more questions regarding his family after that. Maybe she needed to believe it. It made everything much easier.

Grayson turned to leave the office. He could feel her eyes burning into his back. "Investigator Jeffcoat, I will gladly answer your questions tomorrow evening, but I would prefer you not to return to my office. People will get suspicious. No one here knows about my involvement with David, or that I found him in his apartment. The idea of the police snooping around would make everyone apprehensive, and I prefer order in my workplace. Do you understand?" Her voice was tight with a grating air that left a bad taste in Grayson's mouth. He turned around to answer.

"Yes, I understand. You don't want me to come here, and you don't want to come down to the station, which after what I saw today, may not be such a bad idea. Where would you have us meet?" He saw her face draw pensive as she placed her hand on her hip and thought of a suitable place.

"We could meet at Josie's," she said. Josie's was a little deli on the north side of town near David's apartment. "No one would recognize me there. Not this me. I stop in for Pastrami sometimes. It would be inconspicuous." "Ok tomorrow at Josie's, at six o'clock," he replied. "Yes, and Investigator Jeffcoat, I ask that we keep this between ourselves," she replied. "Always," he said as he exited her office.

Grayson smiled at Rebecca as he made his way back through the outer office to the elevators. This case was getting more and more interesting by the minute. You have an heiress, sleeping around on the bad side of town, who claims to be engaged to a man she finds murdered in his own apartment. Grayson was making sure to write all of this down in his notes. He would review them later. He noticed that there were no tears this time, real or crocodile. He would have to do some digging on Jordan Chandler. Something was not right with her. She was cold. Even when she was faking emotion, it felt cold. He had never heard anything about her until a few days ago, and now here she was, dropped in his lap. A mystery inside of a mystery. Grayson was always good at puzzles, but even better at people. He would find out what her problem was, one way or the other. He hoped that tomorrow night would get him some answers or at least get something to point him in the direction of David's killer. That was the most important part of this mystery.

Five

Jordan threw her keys on the coffee table, not caring that it was glass. Today had been a lousy one. It had been one set back after another. The reading of James's will had been bad enough, but the unexpected visit from Investigator Jeffcoat was the icing on the cake. What kind of name was Jeffcoat anyway, she thought as she reached the bar in the far corner of her living room. She quickly downed the first glass of vodka she poured, not even tasting it. She started to pour another but instead decided to take the bottle over to the couch with her. There was no one there to say she couldn't. There hadn't been for a long time. She hated herself when she got like this. Depressed and somewhat desperate. These recent events had taken away from her epic moment in killing David. She had really enjoyed that. She felt so alive afterward for the first time in years. It was exhilarating. Jordan took another sip directly from the bottle and placed it on the table. If her peers could see her now, they'd be laughing their asses off. A waste of an Ivy League education. The Allingtons would immediately have her thrown into some sort of rehab, and the damage control would begin. And what of her father's company? It would be left in the hands of a treacherous slut. Poor Marcus. She could see his face in her mind. He was just a puppet now. Elizabeth used him whenever she wished. She brought him out in public for show when it was necessary, complete with fake adorations just to humiliate him as soon as they were behind closed doors. She hated that bitch.

Jordan sighed, throwing her head back and closing her eyes. She really should have given Marcus some all those years ago. At least he would have had a great memory to hold on to. She laughed aloud.

That brought her to another issue. How would she get rid of Lizzie? It would have to be quick and look accidental. It couldn't be full-on murder. That would be too suspicious. She only had to get rid of her. She didn't mind Marcus. She could learn a lot from him. He would only make the company better, but Lethal Lizzie had to go. "Lethal Lizzie," good one Jordie she thought to herself. She would think more about it later. She had time. Elizabeth Beckett was on her hit list, and that was a place no one wanted to be. Because there was really only one way off. She took another gulp of vodka. She would take care of her in due time.

Jordan reached for her purse to find her cell. She didn't feel like being alone. Maybe she could get Matt to come over. Matt was her former tennis coach. He had taught her many things that didn't require the use of a racket. He reminded her of George Michael, back in his "Freedom" days. She emptied her purse on the table in front of her. Her phone made a loud clang on the table as it fell out. She reached for it coming across Grayson's card. She picked it up and stared at it. Grayson Jeffcoat was very handsome. She wished he wasn't. As much as she thought she would be able to use that against him, she found him to be a bit unnerving. She felt that she may have even underestimated him. She watched him intently during his visit to her office. Nothing about her made him nervous. She was used to intimidating people. That was something she had learned from James. Being his daughter alone made people intimidated. Maybe it was easier because most people she spoke to were employed by her or she had something on them that would make their lives hell if she ever revealed it. He was neither. She would have to be on her "A" game when they met tomorrow night. She had nothing to use as leverage to make him turn the other cheek if he discovered something. She had to make sure he didn't. She lifted the card to her nose. It smelled fresh and clean like the outdoors. She inhaled deeply. She liked that scent. She closed her eyes and imagined her nose being buried in the crook of his neck while she took him in. She felt a tingle in the bottom of her stomach. The scene sickened her. She quickly crushed the card inside her hand and threw it to the other side of the room. I should just kill him, she thought. It's much easier than covering my tracks. But she had never killed a cop, and she didn't plan on doing so now. That would spoil all of her plans. She sat back and began to dial. She needed Matt tonight, even if it was only to pretend he was someone else.

Grayson sat alone at his desk. Most of the officers had gone home. Victoria had left a folder on David Anderson for him. He started flipping through it. Hopefully, something would jump out at him. It didn't. From what he could see, David was a stand-up kind of guy. He had a steady job working as a clerk at a local legal firm. He had only lived in the city for three years. He had moved from the Midwest. Tom had said that their dad was a farmer, and he had expected them to follow suit. That was one of the things that drove David away. He closed the file. He had nothing. No criminal activity to tie David to. Nothing in his file stood out as a reason for someone to kill him. He hadn't lived there long enough to have made any enemies. This wasn't a B&E. Nothing had been taken from what they could see. He had more questions to ask. He would start with David's co-workers and neighbors. Maybe he would get some answers before his meeting tomorrow night. Right now, this was looking mighty personal, and the only person he seemed to be acquainted with on that level was Jordan Chandler. All Grayson knew was that she had a way into the apartment and that she was not sorry he was dead. He was sure of that. But that was all just speculation. No one gets convicted off of hunches.

He thought back to his visit with her. He had to admit, she was trying her hardest to get him away from him, out of his direct line of sight. She would have been fine with never answering any questions. The only time he saw any genuine emotion from her was when he mentioned Tom. She really didn't know that David had any family. That was a shock to her. What kind of people agree to get married and not know anything about each other, Grayson thought. He had to admit he could see why David was attracted to her. She had the perfect hourglass figure. Her eyes were brown like warm honey, and she had the most delicious looking mouth, all plump and luscious. She did her very best to look sterile at work. But even in her stark black business suit, bronze skin glowing as the sun streamed in through the window and her voluminous curls pulled back tightly, she was still attractive. Very attractive. Grayson shook his head. "She is a suspect.......and a bitch," he thought to himself. She is completely off-limits. Apparently, murder, lack of sleep and no sex was turning him into some sort of fiend. He turned off the lamp on his desk and decided to call it a night.

The breeze from the open window stirred Jordan. Her head throbbed.

29

She was naked in bed, the sheet wrapped lazily around her voluptuous form. Matt lay next to her. He was sleeping like a dead man. She liked Matt. He didn't ask questions. He came in, fucked her stupid and left. He never asked for anything else. He knew he didn't have a chance. Jordan wasn't relationship material. She made that clear from the very beginning. She told him upfront if he couldn't deal with it, he was free to leave at any time. He never did. She thought he would have tired of it over these years. He hadn't. He was married and had married people's problems. He welcomed the release. "Hey, Matt," she said, giving him a little push in the side. "Yeah," he replied without turning over. "It's three fifteen. Time for you to get home," she replied. He slowly turned over. "I hate getting up," he said. "We all hate something," Jordan replied. "She will worry." Saying that felt so hypocritical. It really didn't matter if his wife worried. At least not to her. Matt sat up and left his side of the bed, venturing into the adjoining bathroom.

Jordan wrapped the sheet tightly around her and walked over to close the window. She looked out over the skyline. It was beautiful at this time of night. The lights were all brilliant, like Christmastime. As she turned to find her way back to the bed, Matt was exiting the bathroom. He didn't say anything. Neither did she. She never knew what to say at that time. Thank you felt wrong, and anything else would be even more awkward. She guessed words weren't needed. He knew she would call again and he would answer, and that was that.

Jordan stumbled over to the open bathroom door. Matt had left the light on, and she wouldn't be able to get any sleep with it shining onto the bed. As she reached for the light switch, she caught a glimpse of her reflection in the mirror. Her hair was disheveled, eyes bloodshot. Her mascara had run, and there was a lipstick smudge on her cheek. What was she thinking? She had just had sex with a married man and it wasn't the first or last time. And on top of that, Matt wasn't the only one. She peered closer at herself. She had beautiful hair and skin like her mother, but those eyes, those eyes were his. She stood there as if she was willing herself to disappear. She wanted to. She hated James, but she was James. She had become the one thing she hated. She turned out the light, disgusted. She couldn't bear looking at herself a minute longer. She threw herself onto her bed and began to cry real tears for the first time in years.

"Hello," Grayson said into his cell that was lying in bed beside him. "Gray, where are you," asked a familiar voice. "Uh, Vicki……what time is it," he replied. "It's eight thirty. You told me to be here at eight so that we could get the jump on this case," she replied. "Fuck," he replied. "I know what that means," said Vicki. "You are still in bed. You had me haul ass over here, and you are still in the bed." "I'm sorry," replied Grayson. "I'll be right down." "Hey, Gray, I can always come up and help you. I already have an idea of what you look like naked. Let me see if reality is better than fantasy," said Vicki. "It isn't, trust me. You wouldn't like it at all," he replied, laughing. "Did you get my hot chocolate?" "Yeah, I got it, but if you don't hurry your ass down here, I'm going to drink it." "Give me ten minutes, I'll be right there," he replied. "I'll give you five, and then I'm coming up no matter what state of undress you're in," said Vicki. Grayson smiled and hung up the phone.

Vicki looked down at her watch. "Ten minutes exactly." "I told you I'd make it," said Grayson smiling, hair still wet from the shower. "You just didn't want me to see you that's all," she said. "That's probably the fastest you've moved since the Academy." Grayson made no reply but instead reached for his steaming cup of hot chocolate. "And what's up with that anyway," asked Vicki. "Real cops drink coffee." "And so do their stereotypes," said Grayson. "Hot chocolate is better. I don't like the taste of coffee." Vicki looked at him, shrugging her shoulders. "Where to," she asked. "Bailey and Jones, Attorneys at Law. Their office is over on Clements Street." "Ok," she replied as she pressed on the gas and turned the car onto the street, almost causing Grayson to dump his cup in his lap.

Jordan called in and informed Rebecca that she would be working out of her home office this morning. She couldn't go into work looking like this. She was a wreck. She had cried on and off through the night, and there would be no denying it. She sat on the end of her bed. She had a hangover, but what did she expect. She had drunk the entire bottle of vodka before Matt even got there. She believed that it was her way of making everything a little bit easier. He didn't mind that she was drunk. He always just seemed happy to be there. She was using him, and she didn't care at all. He served a purpose. Every person did. His purpose had gone from tennis to fucking, and that was where he would stay unless some other need for him arose.

She felt her legs give a little as she stood. It would be so much easier to crawl up into the center of the bed and cover her head. Or better yet, go downstairs and start on another bottle. Maybe Brandy this time. She reached into her nightstand drawer and pulled out some pain pills. She needed something to stop the aching in her head. It felt like someone was stomping her brain, wearing steel-toed boots. She knew better. Liquor would certainly be her undoing if she didn't get a handle on things. She threw two of the pills into her mouth and swallowed hard. She didn't even bother getting any water. Hopefully, two would be enough. She wasn't sure about taking any more than that after downing the whole bottle of vodka. Even she wasn't that stupid.

Jordan was brought back to reality by the loud ringing of her home telephone, which was really weird because she never used that phone. "Hello," she answered hesitantly. "Oh, Jordie dear, are you feeling alright this morning?" She chilled as she recognized the voice on the other end of the line. "Why are you calling me, and how did you get this number," she asked Elizabeth. "James gave it to me long ago, probably right after you moved out of his home. It was just in case of an emergency. You know, if something were to go wrong," Elizabeth answered. Jordan gritted her teeth. She made a mental note to change the phone number as soon as she ended this call.

"How did you know I was here," she asked. "Oh darling, Rebecca told me," replied Elizabeth. "As partners, I need to be able to speak with you at a moment's notice. I came by your office, and she told me that you were not feeling well today. You're not ill, are you? Or is it something else?" She heard the tone in Elizabeth's voice. She was fishing for something. "I'm just a little under the weather, that's all," answered Jordan. "And you are not my partner, Marcus is." Elizabeth let out a shrill of laughter. "That will soon be rectified," she said coldly.

Jordan didn't like the tone in her voice. "What do you mean, rectified? What are you talking about, Elizabeth? If you harm one hair on Marcus's head, I will..." Jordan had to stop herself. She couldn't make that type of threat, even though she damn well meant it. "My Jordan," she said. "You are getting more and more reckless. Drinking, fucking married men, throwing threats about." Jordan felt her chest tighten. Elizabeth knew about last night. She was watching her. There was a deafening silence on the phone.

"Oh, don't get quiet now, you little cunt," Elizabeth purred into the phone. "Of course, I know. I keep tabs on all my enemies. You are no exception. And as far as Marcus goes, I will provide for him as I see fit. I always do. He is such a fool. Most of them are, even your precious James. He was despicable and morally corrupt, but a fool nonetheless." Jordan felt her blood rising. "Why you," she started, but she heard voices in the background on the other end of the phone. "Coming dear," Elizabeth said, turning her face away from the phone. "I have to go now, Jordie, I hope you feel better," she said in an overly sweet tone as she hung up the phone. That was purely for Marcus's sake since he had entered the room. Elizabeth probably wished she would drop dead immediately.

Jordan slammed the phone down. She hated her. She hadn't quite figured out how she was going to put an end to her, but one thing was for sure, she didn't have time to waste. And what about Marcus? She didn't like what she felt Lizzie was alluding to. There was only one way for them to become partners, and that was only if Marcus were dead. She knew Lizzie was as coldblooded as they came, but she didn't see her resorting to murder. However, if her hands were kept clean in the process, she might chance it. What could she do? She couldn't very well warn Marcus. He wouldn't believe her anyway. He would just say that Lizzie was trying to get her goat. He knew she could never harm him, or so he hoped. Jordan walked over to her bedroom window and looked out. The city was bustling, cars rushing back and forth, people looking like ants. She had a lot on her shoulders. The company, Elizabeth Beckett, this murder and Grayson Jeffcoat. What would she tell him tonight? She had pretty much hoped he would call it off, but she knew that wasn't an option. He was like a dog with a bone, and he wasn't letting up. He would be at Josie's tonight, true to his word.

There was much to do and not much time to do it in. She had to take care of both Grayson and Lizzie, the latter taking precedence. She could more than likely keep Investigator Jeffcoat off her scent for a little longer, but there was immediacy when it came to Lizzie. Not only was she spying on her, but now she was planning to do something drastic to Marcus. She wasn't sure what, but from the tone in her voice, it was something sinister. She had to stop her. She didn't want to share her company with either of them, but definitely not her. Marcus didn't deserve to die at her hands or be left penniless in the gutter while she paraded around town with any one of her gigolos. Jordan decided it was time to get dressed. She had a few people to see to get her plan in motion and six o'clock would be here in a few hours. She at least had to have something solved by then.

Six

Today had been a long day for Grayson. It was just a little past noon, and he had been pounding the streets since this morning. "I thought we would have found out more by now," said Vicki as they walked back to their unmarked car. "Me too," he replied. "No one seemed to know much about David. He seemed well-liked enough by his boss, but other than that, there wasn't much to go on. He kept his personal life private."

"I applaud him," she said. "Everybody knows what everybody does these days. Social media has kind of ruined it."

Grayson laughed. "So, are you putting your life on Facebook, Victoria, if that's your real name?" "I'm on Facebook, and that is my real name," she said. "But it's not my real profile picture. People are crazy these days. Stalkers man, stalkers." Grayson gave her a funny look.

"No one is stalking me," he said. "Jake's my profile picture."

"Jake?" she asked. "That old mutt. He's still alive?" "Yes," Grayson answered. "And if he heard you call him a mutt, he may take a nip at you." "That would be his last day," said Victoria. "Where are we headed to next, Gray?"

"Anderson's apartment," he replied. "Maybe someone there knows something about him or maybe even something about Jordan Chandler."

"Do you think she really had something to do with it," asked Vicki as they pulled on to the road. "I'm not sure," he answered. "But there is something not right about her."

"Her or her involvement in this case?" Vicki asked. "The case, Victoria. The case," he said.

"Ok, well, I was just making sure. You said, "not right about her," and then your eyes did that funny thing."

"What funny thing," he asked.

"You know, when they turn from blue to gray to blue again. That funny thing," she said. Grayson didn't respond. "And now you're quiet. I know what's up." Grayson continued to stare out the passenger side window.

Jordan sat in the back of the mall parking lot. She hated waiting. Lamar knew that. He took his time anyway. She looked at her watch again. Two thirty the dial read. "Damn it," she said, hitting the steering wheel. She heard a tap on her back glass. She looked in her rear-view to see Lamar strolling up on the passenger side. Lamar was a big guy. He was around six foot six and had to weigh at least three hundred fifty pounds, all muscle. He was in the pros once, but an unfortunate accident had sidelined his career. Since that time, he had found more creative ways to make his money. Jordan was one of his benefactors. He was good at what he did. Damn good and above anything else, he was loyal to the one who paid him.

"What's up, Mike," he said, slipping into the passenger seat. He always called her Mike since he discovered her name was Jordan. She had to admit it kind of stuck. It also worked well in situations where he needed to speak to her by phone and didn't have any privacy.

"Lamar, I'm having a bad week," she said. He turned to the side to face her, maneuvering his large frame in the front seat of her car. "What can I do to help you out," he said, flashing his winning smile.

"I have two issues. One is Elizabeth Beckett. The other is this cop."

"Beckett," he said. "That old bitch? I thought you were done with her once James died."

"I thought that too, but James had other plans," she replied.

"So, what do you need? You want her to disappear permanently," Lamar asked. "Yes, but I don't want you to do it per se. I just need your help with clean up." "Ok," he said, nodding. "You're doing it finally, huh?

36

I saw that happening a long time ago. She's got it coming. So how are you gonna do it, and what about her old man?"

"I've not decided yet, and as far as Marcus is concerned, I have no plans of hurting him. But she does," Jordan replied. "I need you to find out what she's planning."

"Okay," Lamar replied. "My brother's company still provides them with drivers. I'll have him keep an ear out. Now, what about this cop?"

"Nothing," she replied. "Forget about him. I can handle him."

"What's his name," Lamar asked. "I can tell you what the streets are saying about him."

"His name is Grayson Jeffcoat."

"Oh, that farm cat," Lamar replied. "He is from the Midwest, pretty fair from what I've heard and strictly by the books. He doesn't suffer from our flaw."

"Our flaw," Jordan asked.

"Lack of integrity," Lamar replied. "He can't be bought. He works his cases to the very end. He's convicted a lot of people." Jordan sighed and bit her bottom lip. "What's he got to do with you, Mike," Lamar asked. "Don't worry about that, big man," she replied. "You will be hearing from me around five."

"Ok, bet," Lamar said. "Same payment plan?" "Same payment plan," Jordan said. "Hit me up," Lamar said as he left her car and slipped back into the shadows of the parking lot.

Jordan sat and watched the people coming in and out of the mall for some time. She was bored but restless. She needed to get this over with. Impromptu killings were not her specialty. She laughed. It wasn't like she was a murderer. Some people just didn't deserve to live. That was the truth. This was always much easier when it was planned, like with David. Her creativity suffered when she had to come up with things on the fly. She was a master in many ways to end a person's life, but she needed something special for Lizzie. It would have to be quicker than she would like, but she would spare her no pain. She owed her. Revenge was a bitch, and tonight, Elizabeth Beckett was going to meet her. Up close and personal.

Grayson knocked on the door of apartment 5G for the second time. "Maybe no one's home, Gray," Victoria said. "Someone's here," he said. "The door is moist, which means something is boiling or producing moisture inside. Whoever it is is cooking. No one leaves boiling pots on."

"Coming," he heard a scratchy voice say. The door opened just a crack with the chain still on at the top. "Who's there," asked a short, balding man with gray hair around the sides of his head.

"Investigators Jeffcoat and Miles," Grayson said, putting his shield up to the crack in the door.

"What do you want," the old man asked. "Mr. Wiesz, we just want to ask you a few questions. Did you know David Anderson?" asked Grayson. Mr. Wiesz pulled his door closed and removed the chain. He stepped in the hall. "Do you mean murdered David, the young man from next door?"

"Yes, sir," Grayson answered. "We just want to find the person who did this."

"Follow me," Mr. Wiesz said, leading them inside of his apartment.

"How can I help you," the old man asked as he sat back in his recliner. "How well did you know David," Grayson asked. "I guess as well as anyone else here. He moved in about a year and a half ago. I would see him coming and going. He was always very polite. I liked that about him. You know most young people nowadays don't have manners," he said.

"Yes, sir," Grayson said.

"See, like you. You have manners." Grayson smiled. "Excuse me," Vicki said. "I don't mean to interrupt, but something smells like it's starting to burn."

38

"It's my stew. I was making dinner for Selma and me," said Mr. Wiesz. "Selma?" Vicki asked. "She's my cat. She's around here somewhere. She's shy."

"I'll turn it off for you."

"It's right through there," Mr. Wiesz said, pointing to a door on the left side of the apartment.

"Is she your girlfriend?" he asked Grayson. "No, she's my partner," Grayson said. "She has kind eyes. My Selma had kind eyes," said the elderly man.

"Your cat?" Grayson asked. "No, my wife, she died ten years ago. The cat reminded me of her, so I called it Selma. I'm not even sure it's female." Grayson smiled kindly at Mr. Wiesz.

"Did you ever see anything weird going on over at David's?" Grayson asked. "No," he answered. "He never had any visitors except her."

"Her?" Grayson asked intently. "Jordan. I think that's her name. Strange name for a girl. She is his fiancée," said Mr. Wiesz.

"How do you know she's his fiancée?" Grayson asked. "He told us. He said she was rich and he was leaving this shit hole, his words, not mine." "Could you describe her?" Grayson asked.

"She is a beautiful girl," Mr. Wiesz said. "She is a beautiful Black woman, like your partner there. She has curly hair and brown eyes. She is about this tall," he said, measuring with his hands. "She had plenty of this and plenty of that. You know, va va va voom, if you get my drift." "Yes, sir, I get it," Grayson said.

"Why if I was a few years younger, I would have stolen her away from him, but I don't think my heart could take it. I know my back couldn't." The two men laughed. "I could always tell when she came to visit, even if I didn't see her."

"How so," Grayson asked.

"She has the sweetest, most peculiar scent. It's like lemons and honey, fresh and sweet. It always lingered in the hallway after she would leave, and there would always be sounds coming from his apartment. You know SOUNDS," the older man said. Grayson dropped his head to continue writing. "I know what you mean," he replied, looking over at Vicki. "But the sounds weren't always good," said Mr. Wiesz. "I'll never forget one night I heard screaming over there. Her screaming. Then there was a door slam a few minutes afterward. The next morning I saw David, he had a band-aid on his left cheek. He said it was a shaving accident. I knew better. He offered up the excuse without me asking first. She started visiting less and less after that. "I see," Grayson said. "Mr. Wiesz, did you see Jordan the other night?" "I did," he replied. "I had come to let Selma back in, and she was there at the door fiddling with her keys. I waved to her, but she didn't wave back. I don't think she saw me. The police came a few minutes after she got here. I was so sorry she had to experience that. She always seemed like a nice girl."

"I see," said Grayson. "Is there anything else you would like to tell us, Mr. Wiesz?"

"That is all I know," he replied. "I hope you catch the bastard who did this. I know something else was going on with David. I have a feeling he was hurting her, using her to move up in the world. But he didn't deserve to die like that. No one does."

"Thank you very much, Mr. Wiesz," said Grayson standing up. "We will call you if we need anything else." Victoria nodded and joined Grayson by the front door. As they headed out, Mr. Wiesz grabbed Grayson's arm. "If I were you, I would make my move. I think she has the hots for you," he said, nodding in Vicki's direction. "Thank you for letting me know," Grayson said, not wanting to hurt the old man's feelings. He gave his arm a pat and joined Victoria in the hallway as Mr. Wiesz shut his apartment door.

"So, what do you make of it," she asked. "Well, from what Mr. Wiesz said, Jordan may have been a victim of domestic violence," answered Grayson.

"But if she was, why would she continue to come back here? She didn't have to," asked Vicki. "Maybe you were wrong after all. Maybe she did love him."

Grayson gave Victoria a thoughtful look. "I highly doubt that. There is something that we're missing here. We just have to find out what it is. I'm going to take another look in his apartment."

"Is it still open?"

"Well, there is only one way to find out," he replied. They moved next door to David's apartment. Grayson turned the doorknob, and it opened. "Let's take a look around. Yell if you find anything suspicious," he told Vicki. "You start in the bedroom, and I'll start here." "Ok, Gray," she said. "Be careful," he replied. He always said that. He knew that they were the only two in the apartment, but it had become a piece of well-worn advice he always felt like giving.

Victoria made her way into the bedroom, and Grayson began scouring the living room. There was something they had overlooked, and he was going to find it.

Seven

It was mostly quiet outside the Beckett house from what Jordan could see. Every now and then, a man dressed all in black would enter and soon leave, then another and another. She drew the conclusion that these were security guards and drivers getting their instructions for the rest of the week. The Beckett's kept a tight rein on security. She didn't think that Marcus had any enemies, but Elizabeth more than likely did. Plus, they were rich, and home invasion was always an option for the less fortunate. She could see Lizzie and Marcus's through their upstairs bedroom window from where they were hiding. Marcus was getting ready for something, and Lizzie was just walking back and forth, waving her hands, running her mouth as usual.

"I don't know why you feel it unnecessary to go to this meeting," said Marcus. "This is a good partnership for the business."

"I could care less about this partnership, Marcus. You know I loathe Jordan," Elizabeth sneered.

"How can you say that, Elizabeth? After all she's been through. After all you've put her through," he said. "I know she hates you, and James making us partners in business was a shrewd move on his part. I don't agree with it, but I know why he did it."

"Do you really?" Elizabeth said. "Do tell."

"James and I had met a few months before he died. He went on and on about how sorry he was for what had transpired between him and me. He said he knew that what he had done could not be forgiven, but he could make it right by making sure that I would be taken care of, at least financially. He was sure that Jordan would not refuse it. The only wild card in the situation was you. He knew that Jordan would not want you near anything that had to do with her. He was almost certain that she would

43

contest the will since there was no way I was going to divorce you. I convinced him that I would make all the decisions and do everything in my power to make sure that your interactions with Jordan were few and far between," said Marcus. Elizabeth sat down on the edge of the bed. "You see, Elizabeth," he continued, "it was not because you had fucked him for many years that he felt like he needed to leave you with something. Why you would think your pussy was worth millions is beyond me. His was a far more gentlemanly deal. He knew that you thought him a fool. The same way you do me. You felt that he was oblivious to your ways. Your REAL ways, but he was not. He felt you deserved nothing. You earned nothing. You knew nothing. You ARE nothing."

"How dare you," she screeched as she slapped Marcus across the face with everything she had. He didn't even flinch. "That my dear proves everything I just said. Be thankful I'm still alive so that you may continue to live this lifestyle because once my eyes are closed, this estate goes to charity, and you will only live off of what Jordan allows." Marcus then picked up the phone. "Randolph, would you please come up and grab my bag? I'm ready. The plane leaves in an hour." Marcus wheeled around Elizabeth as she stood as still as a statue, grabbing his briefcase. "I will return on Tuesday night after my meeting," he said. "Try not to make any more enemies while I'm gone, and please keep your sluttiness confined to the house. I do still have a reputation in this town." Elizabeth didn't say anything. She stomped over to the chaise and threw herself down just as Randolph opened the door.

"Everything is ready, sir," Randolph said, speaking to Marcus.

"Randolph, are you ok, son? You look tired," Marcus asked. "Allergies, sir," Randolph replied. "I've taken something for it." Marcus rolled through the doorway without taking a glance back towards his contemptible wife.

Jordan watched as Randolph and Marcus left the house. She was happy that Marcus wouldn't be there when Lizzie met her demise. She hadn't figured out exactly how she was going to do it yet, and she didn't want to have to silence Marcus too. He was a good man, and she would probably never get over having to senselessly murder him just to cover up his wife's murder. Even she had a code. She never killed anyone she didn't feel deserved it. The only reason she hadn't killed James was that he was her father. That was the only reason. If any other person had done half as many things to her as he had, they would have been over so long ago.

She waited until she found the perfect moment and snuck into the house. She had just made it up the stairs when she heard someone talking coming up the hallway. It was Lizzie. She quickly ducked into the first room she got to. Lucky for her, it was the linen closet. "I know Elliot, but Marcus is such an asshole. I really don't think I can tolerate him much longer, especially after the way he spoke to me today," Elizabeth said into the phone. "I need you to do it and do it quickly." What is she planning to do to Marcus, Jordan thought to herself. And who is Elliot? Jordan heard footsteps coming towards the closet. She quickly stooped down behind a shelf when the door opened. It was one of the maids bringing in fresh towels. She had to get out of there, but not before she figured out exactly what she was going to do. She could still hear Elizabeth. She was on another call now with someone named Derrick. Jordan assumed he was one of her lovers because she was inviting him over for the evening. Jordan had to be out of there before he came.

Jordan peeked out into the dark hallway. She didn't see anyone, so she headed straight for Elizabeth's room. Once she was inside, she heard the shower running. That was her opportunity. Lizzie would never see it coming. She heard the water shut off. She quickly ran into the closet on the left side of the bed. Lucky for Jordan, it was Marcus's. There was plenty of room inside, and she didn't have to worry about Lizzie coming inside. She cracked the door a little and watched as Lizzie withdrew from the bathroom.

She had a towel wrapped around her head, which she threw off as she sat down at her vanity, her dark locks falling over the back of her pink, silk robe. She rubbed cream over her face and topped it off with a few pats of powder. She then slathered her lips with that horrible, red lipstick that Jordan hated so much then sprayed on some perfume from her atomizer.

45

She sauntered over to her armoire and removed a lingerie set complete with garters. Jordan felt as if she might puke. Elizabeth went into the bathroom quickly to return wearing the item. She sat back down at the vanity and began brushing her hair. Jordan covered her face with her mask and slipped out of the dark closet.

She slithered like a snake on her belly around the bed until she was directly behind Elizabeth's chair. She had in her hands the silk tie from her discarded robe. Elizabeth saw the reflection of the figure dressed in black behind her chair and began to scream. Jordan slapped her, immediately knocking her from the chair. Elizabeth tried to crawl towards the bed, but Jordan stopped her. She jumped on her back and held her down. Elizabeth began kicking at her with all her might. Jordan lifted her right leg and broke the ankle with a quickness that Elizabeth let out a horrible scream. Jordan was certain her staff had heard her, but no one came to the door. Jordan flipped Elizabeth over and straddled her.

"What do you want," she screamed. "Money? I have lots of it. If you let me go, I'll give you whatever you want." Jordan just shook her head for no, making sure not to say anything. She wrapped the silk belt around Lizzie's neck. "Please don't do this," Lizzie said. "Don't kill me. Please don't kill me." Jordan looked down at Lizzie as she began to cry, the tears making a path through her powdered face. Jordan held back her laughter and squeezed tighter on the belt. She almost couldn't contain the amount of pleasure this was giving her. Lizzie's eyes began to bulge. This was one of the aspects that she didn't like about strangulation. She didn't like to see this part. "Why…are…you…doing….this," Lizzie got out in her last few breaths. "I...am….a…..good…person." Jordan squeezed tighter on the belt, nearly crushing Elizabeth's windpipe.

"You're not a good person," Jordan said. She saw as Elizabeth was trying to catch her voice. "You're a loathsome bitch," she continued. She saw the shock in Elizabeth's face when she removed her mask. Jordan leaned over to whisper into her ear, allowing her curls to fall forward onto her face. "I owe you this. For my mother, for Marcus, even for James. Tonight, you die, and I want you to remember I did this to you. Let mine be the last face you see." Elizabeth couldn't say anything as Jordan heard her give up what she thought was her last breath. She quickly got up, leaving her body on the floor beside the bed.

Jordan quickly stepped outside the sliding door and immediately began tapping on her cell. "It's done Lamar, how quick can you get here." "About five minutes," he said. "I'm already en route."

"Ok. I strangled her. She is on the left side of the bed. I've been in the linen closet and the bedroom." "I'll sweep them," he said.

"You need to get out of there."

"I will, and Lamar hurry. She had a guest coming. I don't need him to find you there," Jordan said. "Don't worry, Mike, he won't, and if he comes up, I'll take care of it." There was a silence on the line for a second. "Do what you have to," she said. "But we all need to come out clean." "Got it," Lamar said. "I'll call you later tonight." Jordan hung up her phone. She then shimmed to the underside of the balcony and jumped down into the nearest grouping of bushes. She checked her surroundings and scurried to the back wall and went out through the same hole she entered. She ran straight to her car parked in the garage of a house for sale on the next street over.

Jordan made it back to her home safely. She threw herself on to her bed. It was just after five. She laid there looking at the ceiling. Lizzie's dead. It was unbelievable. She played back the scene in her mind. She knew she had done it, but she didn't think she could pull it off. She had really wanted to kill Elizabeth. She could have easily cut her to ribbons, but it would have been too messy. She didn't have time to clean anything up. And Lamar wouldn't have liked all that blood. He hated dealing with blood. She didn't call him after David's murder. The blood looked too good on all that white, and she loved dramatic effects. She pulled herself up to the edge of the bed. She had to get ready. It was about a forty-minute trek to Josie's, and she was sure that Grayson would be on time. She had to clean herself up and get moving. Now to convince him to search somewhere else for his killer, not that she was sure that he had targeted her.

She just had to make certain that he didn't in the near future. She had to admit that she found herself liking Investigator Jeffcoat somewhat. That was why she had decided to let him live. But her mind could be easily swayed based on what happened tonight. Even if she couldn't bring herself to do it, she knew someone who would. She hopped off the bed and headed to the shower.

Eight

"Vicki," have you found anything," Grayson asked, yelling towards the bedroom. "No, everything here is clean," she yelled back. "The only thing that was touched was his unmade bed, which I'm sure he had gotten out of before he was murdered."

"There was something else strange about it, though," she said, walking out of the bedroom. "What's that," Grayson asked. "There was no sign of her here," she said.

"What do you mean?"

"She didn't leave any of her clothes, no toiletries, not even a toothbrush. This was all I found," said Victoria holding up a white linen handkerchief with lace trim. "Well, maybe she didn't stay over a lot and plus if she was coming from a dance class, she had probably showered there and had a bag with her," Grayson said. "That makes sense, I guess," said Victoria.

"So, anything else feels funny to you," he asked. "Nothing other than this smell," she said. "Smell right here. It's very lemony like someone had done some cleaning." Grayson sniffed the air.

"It's too sweet for that," he said. "It smells like her."

"Her?" Vicki asked. "Remember, Mr. Wiesz said that she smelled lemony," Grayson replied. "The smell is strong here, but she was nowhere in this area when I arrived. She wouldn't even go near the body. This smell is pretty strong for something that happened days ago," she said.

"Do you think she's been back here?" Grayson looked around the room quickly. There is no way that he could tell if she had been there or not. Her prints, of course, were there because upon her own admittance and

49

the neighbors, she spent a great deal of time at the apartment. She was even there on the day of the murder. "There's no way for me to tell," he said. "But I will do some snooping. She may give something away when I see her tonight." "You're seeing her tonight," she asked. "To answer my questions, that's all," he said. "This was the only way she would agree to it. I'm actually due at Josie's in a few minutes." "Well, let's go if we're done here," said Victoria. "We're done," said Grayson closing the apartment door.

Jordan walked down Nichols Street gingerly. She would be meeting with Grayson in just a few minutes. She really wasn't feeling it, but she had to be there. She had put him off once already, and she knew if she didn't go tonight, he would more than likely haul her ass down to the station tomorrow without any reservations. She had dressed quickly, wearing jeans and boots, a black turtleneck and a pea coat. Her hair was down falling around her shoulders. She was hoping to look somewhat innocent, or at least as innocent as she could portray. She wondered what kind of questions Grayson would ask. Would she be willing to answer them? She wasn't sure about that. She didn't regret either of the murders, but she didn't like to be questioned. That was just something that wasn't about to take up a lot of her time. She just wanted to get there and get it over with. Just as soon as she reached her destination, she felt her pocket vibrate.

She took out her phone. It was Lamar. Jordan quickly surveyed her surroundings and backed into the alleyway next to Josie's. "Yes," she answered into the phone. "Hey, Mike, just wanted to let you know everything was taken care of. Man, what a number you did on her."

"That's good, Lamar. Did you get everywhere?" "Yeah, the bedroom, bathroom, and linen closet," he replied. "Did anyone see you," she asked. "No, but her boy toy did arrive a few minutes after I was done. I had to hide in the bathroom. You should have seen him. He was all over her crying. He was trying to unwrap the belt from around her neck, but you had bound it way too tight."

"Where is he now," she asked. "The cops have him," Lamar answered. "Wait, the cops, how," she asked. "When he was doing all his crying, I called and said that I heard a woman screaming at this address. They were here in no time," he replied. "They caught him red-handed. His fingerprints were on everything, including her."

"And none of this can be traced to you? Are you sure, Lamar?" she questioned. "Positive, Mike. I used one of the burners I have on me at all times. I had to wait for them to haul him away before I could leave, which was much easier than getting in after the mess the cops were making." "Cool," she said. "I'll catch up with you on Saturday morning." "Bet," he said, hanging up. Jordan stepped out of the alleyway and continued on to Josie's.

Grayson watched Jordan raptly. She never even noticed him sitting in his truck across the street. He wondered why she stepped into the alleyway to answer her call. He knew it was a call because he saw her take the phone from her pocket. She didn't seem afraid of getting mugged. She shot into the alley immediately, even though it was dark, and anyone could have been lurking inside. When she appeared again, she looked somewhat cooler, less nervous. Maybe it was a good call. Maybe it was something to do with this case. He rolled up his window. It really didn't have to have anything to do with this case. Maybe she had gotten a call and stepped into the alley to hear better. But what rich heiress steps into dark alleys unaccompanied. Apparently, one who was familiar with that type of thing? He locked his truck and moved across the street. He had worn jeans and a simple Henley topped with a light jacket. He needed to fit in and not look so "cop-ish." He made sure his badge and gun were both concealed inside of his jacket. He had better hurry because he had a feeling if Jordan Chandler was left alone for more than five minutes, she would bolt, and there would be no getting any answers out of her after that. He looked in the window and saw her sitting in a booth not too far from the front entrance.

Josie's was your typical corner deli. It had black stools with chrome legs, which were lined around a long counter that seemed to reach from the front entrance to the middle of the diner. The floor was tiled in black and white squares, and the booths were huge with red, leather seats. It reminded Grayson of something out of the fifties. He was certain that his parents would enjoy the atmosphere. It had a very distinct smell, one of freshly cut meats tinged with the sweet scent of milkshakes and malts that they made as desserts along with baked goods like sour cream pound cake and apple pie.

"Hi," he said as he reached Jordan's booth. "May I sit down?" Jordan didn't say anything. She just motioned with her hand to the seat on the other side of the booth. "I expected to find you here waiting," she said as Grayson took his seat. "Normally, I would have been early, but I had a lead to chase. You know, police work," he replied.

"So how was your evening so far, Ms. Chandler," he asked. "We didn't come here for polite conversation, Investigator. Please get on with your questions," she said. Grayson just stared at her. She didn't blink. She didn't seem uneasy. Clearly, she felt that she was in control of the situation. "Well, Ms. Chandler, I did think that a person of your standing would appreciate niceties, but since you are content on being as rude as possible, I will make this as quick and unpleasant as I can."

Now, she did the staring. "Investigator Jeffcoat," she started, "if I seem rude, I do apologize. It is just that this has been a difficult time for me. I've not had time to grieve, and I just want to get this over with." He saw something in those brown eyes that made him feel a little sympathy for her. "I understand, Ms. Chandler. I don't mean to seem pushy, but your answers are pertinent to this investigation. I'm sorry for your losses, both David and your father. I want this done as quickly as you do. And again, you can call me Grayson," he said, taking the notepad from his jacket pocket.

She smiled at him. Her mouth was pure decadence, he thought to himself. Her lips were far too pouty and perfect to speak anything good. "Grayson," she said in her sweet throaty voice, "thank you for your concern. You may ask your questions. I promise not to interrupt." He heard what she said, but he had a hard time tearing his eyes away from her mouth. "Grayson," she said again. "Are you okay?" Grayson snapped back to reality.

"Yes, Ms. Chandler. I'm fine. Sorry about that, sometimes there is a lot going on in my head." "I imagine so," she replied, "and please call me Jordan." Grayson smiled. Jordan felt her heart flip. He had the most handsome face, rugged and chiseled with dimples and about two days' worth of stubble. His hair was black as a raven's wing, and his eyes were a bluish-gray or grayish-blue depending on which way the light hit. She really wondered why he was a cop. He could make easy money on his looks alone.

"Ok, well, Jordan, how well did you know the deceased," Grayson asked. "I've known David about a year and a half now. I guess it was a type of love at first sight thing," she said.

"How did you meet?" "He was actually walking past the dance studio one night, and I ran into him. Literally," she said. "Go on," Grayson urged. "I was in a rush to get to my car. I had a meeting to go to, and it was with a client I really hated. So, I came to class just to let off some steam before. I was walking down the sidewalk, not really paying attention, fiddling in my bag for my keys and bumped into him." She laughed. Her laugh was peculiar but beautiful. "You should have seen his face. He asked me out that very night. I, of course, said no, but he was relentless. Every time I left dance class, he would be there waiting to ask me again. I eventually gave in. It was so much fun. We went to movies, dinners, museums, all over the place. It was nice to be with someone who didn't want something from me," she said as she beamed. Grayson knew that was not true. David had told Mr. Wiesz that Jordan was his ticket out. Whether she knew it or not, he didn't burst her bubble. He just moved on to the next question.

"How long had you all been engaged," he asked. "For about six months. David was saving to buy me a ring. I thought that was cute. I didn't need one, but he was very traditional about the whole thing," she said. "I see," he replied. "We were so in love. Have you ever been in love, Grayson?"

"Pardon me," the waitress interrupted. She had appeared at the booth without being noticed. "Can I get you two anything?"

"Black coffee for me," Jordan said. "Hot chocolate for me," said

Grayson. Jordan just gave him a strange look. "It's a long story," he said, smiling. "Hey, I understand. No judging," she replied. She laughed again. "I'll get it right out," the waitress replied. Her brown hair encased tightly in a hair net as she turned her back to walk back to the kitchen.

"It's getting warm in here," Jordan said, taking her coat off. The black turtleneck was fitting snugly on her curves—her ample bosom stretching the material to its limits. Grayson hastily tried to find somewhere else to focus his gaze. He, too, removed his jacket. The room had just gotten hotter to him too. The waitress reappeared with their drinks and placed them on the table.

"You never answered," Jordan said.

"Answered what?" Grayson replied.

"My question," she started. "Have you ever been in love?" Grayson lifted his cup to his lips. "No," he said over the steam. Jordan just looked at him with those gorgeous sable eyes. "Pity," she said. "It's wonderful." Grayson smiled again. "I'm asking the questions here," he said. "Touché," she replied, taking a sip of her coffee.

"Jordan, did you know anyone who would want to harm David. Did he have any enemies?"

"I don't think so," she replied. "David always seemed kind of happy go lucky to me."

"Okay," Grayson replied. "Do you think someone would have wanted to hurt him to get to you?"

"No, that would have been highly unlikely," she replied.

"Why do you say that," he asked. "Very few people knew about David and me," she said. "My own father didn't know. He would have never approved." She glanced down at her cup. "Your father was very protective of you, I would imagine," Grayson said.

"Not really," she replied. "He just didn't like outsiders. People who were not on our level. He felt that they were only good at manipulation. They would only be out for what they could get. David wasn't like that." Grayson found himself feeling sorry for her. She honestly thought that David loved her. It was sad. He had heard about the rich never having people that cared about them, and they would grasp at anyone who showed them attention. They were virtually starving for love. He hated to think that Jordan was like that. Just from sitting across the booth from her, he knew she could have any man she wanted.

"Jordan, did David ever hit you," Grayson said without any warning. He saw her hand shake a little as she lowered her coffee cup to the saucer. "No," she said softly, her eyes not meeting his. "I'm sorry if these questions make you uncomfortable. We are just trying to figure out what type of guy Anderson was. That would give us some indication of why someone would murder him."

"I understand," she said, regaining her composure. "Why would you assume that?"

"Well, we have interviewed some of David's neighbors. They said they heard female screams coming from his apartment," he said. "Then they said you pretty much stopped coming around. Was he violent?"

"David would never hurt me," she interjected. "He just would get angry sometimes, that's all. He never meant anything by it. The hurt never really lasted." Grayson just looked at her. He didn't like the idea that David Anderson had put his hands on her. He couldn't believe that she had allowed that. He was hoping that the disbelief didn't show on his face.

"I'm sorry that happened to you," he said. "You know you can talk to someone about that." He saw her face harden just a little bit. "I don't need to talk to anyone," she said. "I'm fine. What's done is done." Grayson wanted to reach out and hold her. He saw the misery in her eyes. "Is that all," she asked. "Yes, that's all," Grayson replied. "Thank you for your time." She reached in her purse to pay for her coffee. "Don't worry about it," he said, putting some money on the table for both of them. She grabbed her coat and slid out of the booth.

55

"I'll walk you to your car," he said, scrambling after her. She didn't even look back. "Hey, what did I say," Grayson said hurrying behind her. "You didn't do anything," she said, looking back at him for just a second. He could see the tears streaming down her face. Why was she crying?

"Hey, Jordan," he screamed as she crossed the street to the parking lot. He ran out into the street, not looking at what was coming. Cars in both lanes were honking their horns as he crossed into the parking lot. "What's wrong," he said, grabbing her arm just as she reached her car. She winced as he spun her around. "Are you okay?" he asked. "What happened to your arm? Did he do that to you?"

"I'm fine. Just fine. Let me go and leave me alone," she said. "I've answered all of your questions, now let me go." Grayson let go of her. "I really didn't mean to upset you back there, Jordan, but I have to do my job. I'm really sorry." She just stood there with her head down, tears dropping on the ground between their feet. He reached for her pulling her into his arms. He knew it was unprofessional. He knew it was wrong. But there she was crying in front of him and needing someone to offer some kind of comfort. He'd be damned if he wouldn't oblige.

She didn't pull away from him. He knew that she was crying harder from the way her body shook in his arms and the amount of wetness that was soaking through his shirt. Mr. Wiesz was right, she did smell lemony sweet. He stood there and inhaled the scent as he held her, his chin resting on the top of her head. He had to admit. It felt good. She felt good. Her curves molded against him, and as much as he tried to reason with his body, some of its parts had its own ideas. She released him, no doubt feeling the strong but silent intruder who made his presence known between their bodies.

"I'm sorry," she said. "You must think I'm an idiot falling apart like that."

"Don't worry about it," he said, assuring her. "It happens to the best of us. I cried at Bambi." She laughed. "See, it all comes back," he said, referring to her smile. "Do you need me to call someone for you? I'm certain you have drivers on standby."

"No, I'm fine," she replied, opening her car door. "Are you ok," she asked him. Grayson smiled that billion-dollar smile again, and she was lost. "Yeah, I'm fine," he said. "I'm sure I can make it home." She knew he was being sarcastic. "Grayson," she called out to him as he was walking away. "Yeah," he said, turning in her direction. "Thank you again," she said as she was in an arm's length of him before he knew it. "No problem," he said. "Thank you for answering my questions."

Before he could say anything else, Jordan Chandler was kissing him. She had caught him off guard. He wanted to push her away, but he couldn't bring himself to do it. Her lips were so soft he couldn't resist it. She was aggressive with her kiss, not like he would have expected. She ran her tongue across his bottom lip and nibbled it a little to demand entrance. He gasped a little, and she took full advantage, forcing her tongue into his mouth, finding his and entrancing it in a dance he had never felt before. He felt like he was falling. He could hardly catch his breath. Then she released him.

She looked him squarely in the eye. He had almost expected her to have a look of embarrassment. He thought that she would shyly say she was sorry and ask him to forgive her; she was caught up in the moment. She did neither. She made no apologies. "Right now, your eyes look more gray than blue. I think I'll call you Gray, Investigator Jeffcoat." She gave a seductive smile. She wasn't sorry one bit.

"Victoria always does," he said, looking down at her. "Victoria?" she said suspiciously. "She's my partner and the second-best investigator I know," he said sarcastically. Jordan smiled again. "I'll keep that in mind." She reached into her purse and grabbed her handkerchief to dry her eyes. "I am sorry about that," she said, pointing to the front of his shirt. "It will dry," he said. "The heat in my truck is great." She looked at him as if she wanted to say more, but she didn't.

"I'll contact you if we have more questions," he said as he turned to walk away. "Please do," Jordan replied. "And thank you again, Gray. For everything." "No problem," he said as he crossed the street, making sure to look both ways this time. Jordan watched as Grayson crossed and continued back up the block towards the deli. She laughed to herself. That's how you control a situation, she thought. Grayson Jeffcoat would be putty in her hands now. She got in her car and drove off, admitting to herself that she had enjoyed it as much as he did.

Nine

Grayson pulled into his driveway. He felt as if he hadn't been home in ages. That was the one thing he hated about being a cop—long hours. He heard the familiar sound of his best friend's bark. He was so happy that he was able to find a home that was out in the country. His dog needed the open air. "Hey there, boy," he said, rubbing his head as the collie came bounding through the front door. He gave him a couple of pats on the head before he took off for the yard. Grayson made himself comfortable on the couch and clicked on the television. He didn't like TV that much, but it was a great distraction from his real life. He just made sure he didn't watch any cop shows. Most of them had everything wrong. That also seemed the case with law shows too. That's why the American public felt like they could solve their own cases—a serious case of too much TV. He flipped through the channels but couldn't find anything to hold his interest. There was nothing good on the sports station, and the news was not an option for winding down.

He placed his hands behind his head and leaned back on the couch, closing his eyes. He saw Jordan's face. Her eyes looking into his, her lips parting for that kiss. Why did he let her do that? He knew no good would come of it. He knew it, but he couldn't stop himself. He knew more than likely that would be his only opportunity. If she hadn't been so emotional, it wouldn't have happened anyway. He had to admit that he loved the way her body fit up against him. She made soft moans when she kissed, which had the ability to drive a man insane. She smelled like a lemon pastry, all sweet and sugary, but tart and fresh on the insides. What am I doing, he thought. I've lost it, comparing women to pastry. He felt his body stir in that all too familiar place and quickly sat upright. This was crazy. It was just a kiss. But he had to admit it was the best kiss he had had in a lifetime and from a rich, beautiful, available woman, whom he could not touch again if he valued his job or reputation.

Grayson got up off the couch. He needed a shower. A shower would solve all his problems. No, it wouldn't really, but it would solve the one that was most pressing at this time. And once that was solved, he could better concentrate on any other issues at hand. He walked into his bedroom and emptied his pockets on the dresser. He put his gun in the nightstand drawer, and laid his phone on top, grabbed a towel and headed towards the door in the far corner of the room, which led into his bathroom. He needed to get himself together. He didn't even see the glow from his phone screen as it vibrated on the nightstand. Someone was calling, but right now, he didn't seem to care who.

The limousine skidded around the curve like it was rolling on glass. Marcus woke up in a panic. He looked down at his watch. He had fallen asleep some time ago since Randolph wasn't doing any talking. He was shocked at the amount of time that had passed. He thought that he had surely missed his plane since they weren't anywhere near the airport yet. "Randolph," he said, pressing the intercom button. He didn't receive a reply. "Randolph, please lower the partition," he said. Still no response. "Randolph…Randolph……RANDOLPH," he continued to shout. There was nothing. The car veered off to the right. It soon ran off the road into a nearby patch of trees. What was happening? Randolph had lost control of the car. Marcus could see that they were going entirely too fast by the way the trees were passing his semi-tinted windows. He found himself being jostled about in the back seats. "RANDOLPH," he shouted one last time before giving up. Apparently, Randolph had lost consciousness. Marcus fell out of his seat. Just as he attempted to pull himself back up, he heard a loud deafening sound. He knew in that moment it was over. The car began to flip over and over. It finally came to a stop with a loud boom, standing upright against a tree.

Jordan pranced around her bedroom, feeling mighty proud of herself. Tonight she had accomplished two major things; one getting rid of Elizabeth Beckett once and for all and two getting her hooks into Grayson Jeffcoat. She was certain that she was in his head now, and if she played her cards right, she could control this whole investigation and make certain he never considered her if he happened to get on Lizzie's case. She smiled. She did have to admit that kissing Grayson wasn't just a ploy. She was dying to know what it felt like. He was her type of man, and if he wasn't investigating this murder, she would certainly consider dallying with him. After all, why not? He wouldn't require much, and he would be gone most of the time, leaving her to all her other trivialities. She did enjoy their conversation, though. He was smart, thoughtful and funny—any girl's dream, but she wasn't any girl and she didn't dream. Her psyche catered to nightmares. That was the problem. She jumped into the middle of the bed, grabbing the pint of Hagen-Daz she had nabbed from the kitchen and turned on her TV. Tonight they were showing her favorite movie, Queen Bee, with Joan Crawford. She adored Joan Crawford. She was always so no-nonsense in her roles. She made the men stand back and take notice, and she didn't have a problem with working every angle or using everything she had to get the outcome she desired. That was her kind of role model.

Should she call him, she thought to herself. No, that's rushing it. Her movie started as she stuffed spoonfuls of ice cream into her mouth. He would think she was desperate. She wasn't. She could call a number of men over right now, but none of them could be used in that capacity, and none of them were Grayson. She had a sick little need inside her to possess him, even if it was only once. She would have Grayson Jeffcoat, would know the feel of his arms and the mold of his hard, swollen dick inside her. She wanted that and from his reaction to her, he wanted it too. She would be more than happy to give it to him, but she couldn't rush it. He was no fool. He would know she was up to something. Everything had to go according to plan, her carefully crafted plan.

She leaned back on her pillow and closed her eyes. His lips were so soft, his mouth so warm. She hadn't been kissed in a long time, a very long time. She didn't allow her friends to kiss her. It was too personal, and she wasn't on that type of level with them. Sure, sex was intimate, but not personal. There was a difference. Sex satiated a need. It was basically an unfeeling act. Sure, she felt the normal physical attributes of enjoying a sexual experience, but inside was blank, void. That is what kept it from becoming personal. Personal involved feelings, and she just didn't have those to give. Maybe that was something Grayson could help her with, but not now. She had to get her ducks in a row and plus how could she find herself falling in love with a cop when she planned on continuing in her ways. Murder assholes first and then go home and make it with a cop. Hmmmmm, she laughed to herself. That was something Joan would do. She would fuck him shitless, make him love her and then either kill him herself or throw herself at his mercy to save her at the end of the film. Either way, it's classic bad, and she loved the classics. She just wasn't sure how she would play it yet, but either way would work for her.

She felt the familiar wetness building between her thighs. She should call someone to take care of that, but she opted out. That would ruin her movie and probably her mood. She dipped her hand inside her pants. She would just take care of it herself. It would be much easier and safer. She threw her head back as she began to enjoy the melody that her fingers were strumming. This was sometimes better to her, at least it was more pleasing because you didn't have to deal with the aftermath. Her friends knew it was no strings attached, but she knew a few of them found themselves being drawn to her, wanting relationships. She didn't want that. She had no inclination of wanting to be tied down. That wasn't for her. She stopped her ministrations to grab a sip from her glass of vodka that she had placed on the nightstand. Overall, tonight was a success. She had done everything she had set out to do, and now her favorite movie was on to boot. She had done well today. This is what made her feel successful. It had nothing to do with business. She placed the glass back down and continued with what was making her feel the absolute best, while Joan played out in the background.

That shower did Grayson a lot of good. He felt much clearer as he left his bathroom. He thought that he may finally get a chance to make a home-cooked meal tonight. He hadn't done so in a while. He was never really at home. He had made a life pretty much of junk food these days, and he could feel it. He was just lucky that it hadn't begun to show on the outside of his body. There was a chill as he entered his bedroom. He liked his showers hot, so there was a fierce difference in temperatures when he entered the bedroom. Even more so since he was wearing just a towel. He headed over to his dresser to grab a T-shirt when he noticed the familiar glow of his phone on the nightstand. "Three missed calls," it glared. He touched the screen to see what he'd missed. Three calls from Victoria. That was weird. He knew something had to be up because she never called like that. He quickly hit redial.

"Hey, Vicki, what's up," he said into the phone when she picked up. "Sorry I missed your calls. I was in the shower."

"Yeah, yeah, pretty boy," she started. "Look, I need you to get your ass down here." "Down where," he said. "3478 Witcomb, the Beckett estate," she replied.

"Beckett," he asked, "as in Marcus and Elizabeth Beckett."

"Yes," she replied. "Mrs. Beckett has been knocked off."

"WHAT," he said. "When? How?" "She was strangled apparently by her lover," said Vicki.

"Lover?" asked Grayson. "What about Mr. Beckett?" "Not here," she replied. "He left yesterday on a business trip. No one has been able to contact him." "You don't think he's in on it, do you?" "No, this guy was caught red-handed." "Anything else special,'" he asked. "Not sure. That's why I need you. Hurry up," she screamed into the phone. "I'm on it," he said, hanging up.

Ten

By the time Grayson got there, the estate was swarming with police and reporters. "Not this again," he thought to himself. Every time some big wig was involved in something, these reporters crept out the woodwork like extras from the Thriller video. And what made it even worse is that someone here had been murdered, but they could care less. It was a media frenzy outside the house. He had to almost barge his way in.

"Hey," he said, walking towards Victoria. "Hey yourself," she replied. "So, what have you found out so far," he asked.

"Well, not so much. Mrs. Beckett was found there," she said, pointing to a spot on the floor. "She had the belt to her silk robe wrapped around her neck and pulled tight for effect."

"You said the suspect was apprehended on the scene," Grayson asked. "Yeah, some young tough," she said. "Forrester said he had the silk tie wrapped around his hands when he burst in the door. He said the dude looked like a deer in headlights."

"Who called it in," he asked. "I'm not sure," she replied. "Dispatch said it was reported by someone on the grounds, but everyone we've questioned so far said that they didn't make the call or see anyone."

"Still no word on Mr. Beckett," Grayson asked.

"No, and it's really strange. According to the staff, Marcus Beckett can always be reached when he isn't here. He didn't suffer the idea that being gone from home meant disappearing. He liked to be kept abreast of everything that was happening around his home and family." Grayson just gave the room a cursory glance. There were too many people for him to really be able to check into anything. "I hope that Mr. Beckett contacts this place soon. This isn't something a man should come home to without being made aware," he said. "True, but we can't wait around here for that," said

65

Victoria. "At least both of us can't."

"Who's keeping an eye on our suspect," Grayson asked. "They just took him down to the station," she replied. "I asked them to put him in Interrogation Room 4. I knew one of us would be down there soon enough."

"Do we have anything to hold him on other than the fact that he was here," Grayson asked. "Well, he was here. He was found with the murder weapon in his hand and he was well acquainted with the victim," said Vicki.

"That's about it. What's his story?" he asked. "You know, the regular. He had come in for a visit and found her on the floor. He said he was trying to unwrap the belt, but we aren't certain about that," she said.

"So, you're holding him on suspicion," asked Grayson. "We aren't sure of anything yet, Gray," she replied. "We haven't had time to run his record. It was hard enough trying to get him out of here. Too bad for Mrs. B, though."

"What do you mean," Grayson asked. "You mean something other than being dead?"

"She had just become a whole lot richer," she replied. "How so," Grayson asked. "Well, her ex-lover left her and her husband half of his company in his will," she replied.

"Her ex-lover," he asked. "and her husband went along with this."

"Back in the day, they were all friends, or at least that's what the tabloids say. But you could ask your other suspect about it."

"My OTHER suspect?" he said, looking at her quizzically. "Yeah, from your murder case, Jordan Chandler. It was her father who left it to them," she said.

"Fuck," Grayson said. "So, you're saying someone else who was close to her is dead."

"Seems that way," Victoria said. "You always look so cute when you cuss, Gray," she said, squeezing his arm. "Maybe your girlfriend is a black widow."

"She's not my girlfriend, and I highly doubt she's a black widow," he said. "I'm just saying this is the third person from her life that has died here recently. It's just kind of creepy. You may need to stay clear of her," said Victoria. Grayson laughed.

"First of all, it's not like she and I are hanging out. We just met so that she could answer some questions for me. Secondly, you're not my mom, so you can't really tell me who to hang out with," he said.

"Alright, no need to get defensive. I'm just looking out for your ass," she said. "You know how things get when you start thinking with your little head." He didn't even justify that comment with a response. "We've done all we can do here. Let's head down to the station and see what we can find out," she said. "Ok, I just have to make one quick call first," he said. "Do what you gotta do, man. I'll be outside," Victoria said, leaving the bedroom.

Jordan could feel her phone vibrating somewhere on the bed even though she couldn't see it. She found it underneath a pillow at the foot of the bed. "Hello," she said. Her speech noticeably slurred. "Hey, this is Grayson," said the voice on the other end of the phone. "Oh, hey you," she said into the cell. "What are you up to? I was thinking about you." He noticed what she said, and he almost found himself wanting to ask was that the truth.

"Jordan, are you ok," he said. "You don't sound like yourself."

"I do sound like myself," she said back into the phone. "I sound like my drunk self," she said with a giggle. "What is it, Gray," she slurred. "Well, I have some news for you, but it can wait until tomorrow," he said.

"Are you going to come over tonight," she asked, still giggling into the phone. "I've been having naughty thoughts about you and touching myself. Do you want to touch me?" Grayson couldn't believe what she was saying. Not only was she drunk, but she was also out of her gourd. He wanted her to keep talking because he found himself aroused by what she was saying.

But he also knew she wasn't thinking straight, so what was the point.

"Gray, are you there? You didn't answer my question," she said. "Never mind, Jordan. I'll just tell you in the morning," he said. "Tell me in the morning, tell me in the morning," she kept chanting. He couldn't help but laugh. "We will talk tomorrow," he said into the phone. He could tell by her voice that that was not what she did want to happen."

"We could talk now in the flesh," she purred into the phone. "I'm already in mine," she said, laughing seductively. That laugh brought life to another phase of his personality. "I have to go now, Jordan," he said. "I'll call tomorrow," he said. "Fine," she sneered. "Suit yourself. Joan and I will enjoy the rest of the night. Isn't that right Joan," she said. "Joan," he asked. "Who's Joan?" "Joan Crawford, you silly willy," she said. Grayson just shook his head. "I'll see you tomorrow Jordan and drink lots of coffee," he said. She just giggled and hung up the phone.

When Grayson returned home, he could barely keep his eyes open. He was so tired it was hard to think straight, but one thing was certain—there was something wrong with Jordan Chandler. Not wrong per se, as if she was mentally ill, but it was the fact that she seemed very lonely. She could be hot one minute and cold the next, and even though she didn't tell him so, he knew that she was drunk. And he was certain this was something else she was good at. He plopped down on the side of his bed to remove his shoes when an oh so familiar voice entered his head. *"I've been having naughty thoughts about you and touching myself. Do you want to touch me,"* it said. "Damn right, I wanna touch you," he thought to himself. Jordan was hungry for attention, and he was dying to give it to her. He was starving himself. If only she wasn't drunk, he thought. Shaking his head, he lay back on his pillows and closed his eyes. He disciplined himself quickly because he knew where his mind was heading. It wasn't a secret. He had to maintain control of it if he ever planned on getting to the bottom of this murder. These murders, he corrected—two back to back and both of them having to do with her. Or let's say involving people that she was acquainted with. He really didn't want to go along with Victoria's Black Widow theory. It just didn't make any sense. Besides, Jordan couldn't kill anybody. He could see those beautiful eyes in his mind and those pillow-soft lips. She couldn't kill anyone. She would probably be a blubbering mess, crying all over the place. That thought brought a smile to his face. Not that he enjoyed seeing her cry, but the fact that her heart was too tender to commit cold-blooded murder. That made him feel much better. He chose to believe that. He pulled the blanket up over his shoulders and drifted off.

Jordan woke up early the next morning. She found her ice cream carton turned over on the side of the bed. No worries, though. She knew it was empty. She actually remembered devouring the last bite of it right before Joan drove off the road. Joan Crawford was a beast. She laughed out loud. She did some acting on her own, often on a daily basis. She sat upright and clicked on the television. Just as she thought, the major headline on every station was the death of Elizabeth Beckett. "Well, Lizzie, I've continued your notoriety," she said. "Even in death, you're all the rage." She slid her feet over the side of the bed, allowing her toes to sink into the plush carpet. No slippers were waiting. She had no idea where she had kicked them off. She stood, stretching, while the news was going on and on about Lizzie and her wealth and philanthropy. None of which actually belonged to her, not truly. From what Jordan had heard her father say, Elizabeth was one of those girls from the wrong side of the tracks. She happened to just possess enough audacity to think she belonged in their world and just the amount of gumption to pull it off. Marcus had fallen in love with her on sight. It must have been her hair, thought Jordan. I did admire that about her. Her personality, however, was bitter as gall. She was definitely not a likable person. Jordan wondered what Marcus was going through. She felt for him in all of a minute. He really loved old Lizzie. He was the only one, and because of that, he would be the only one to mourn her. Alone, but finally free of her. Jordan grabbed her phone and headed for the bathroom door only to look down and see that she had taken a call from Grayson.

Shocked filled her briefly. She didn't remember talking to Grayson. She had no idea what she may have said to him. She was normally quick, thinking on her feet, but last night she was drunk. She had allowed her celebration to go to the extreme. How can I find out what I said, she thought to herself. She couldn't find out without asking him. The more she thought about it, the more she got upset. She may have said anything. Did she confess to either of the murders or both? She felt her knees buckle. She looked over at the empty vodka bottle on the nightstand and vowed to never drink again. She made that vow every time she had one of these nights. She knew she was just talking to hear herself talk. She would have one of these nights again. Maybe even tonight. She glanced up at the television when she heard them say the name of the suspect in Lizzie's murder. Derrick Delgado. He looked absolutely terrified in his mug shot. The news reporter said that Delgado was a known high-end escort and that he had been arrested a few times for prostitution when he first moved to town, but other than that, he had no record of criminal activity. Jordan frowned. He may get off. He wasn't a hardened criminal by any means, and all the cops had was circumstantial evidence. If Delgado was able to find himself a good lawyer, he could be out as early as today, she thought. She was going to have to find some way of making it stick. As long as they had Delgado, they weren't looking for her. She let out a sigh and an easy smile. She felt a little bit better already. She flipped off the television, threw the remote on the bed and headed for the bathroom.

Eleven

"I thought you'd never get here," Victoria said to Grayson as he reached his desk. "Well, good morning to you too, Ms. Victoria," he said sarcastically. "Sorry, but I've got news," she said. "What did you find out," he asked. "How did the interrogation go?"

"It went fine. But we didn't discover much. He still says he's innocent. I hate to admit it, but I believe him. He admits that he's her "boy toy." He makes regular visits there, and she pays him well. They hadn't had a falling out, and he had just spoken to her about two hours before she was murdered. We verified that on his cell. He has no history of violence, and he seems to be more of a wuss, if you get my meaning. He is more of a house cat. Totally tamed," she said. Grayson just ran his hand through his hair.

"Well, you said you had news, what's up," he said. "I'm not sure you're going to like it," said Victoria. "Why wouldn't I like it," he asked. "What does it have to do with me?" Victoria gave him a look he knew far too well. One he actually hated. "It may tie in to your case," she said, walking over to her desk. "You think the person who killed Jordan's fiancé killed Elizabeth Beckett," asked Grayson.

"I didn't say that," she replied. "But what I am saying is that someone who was in that apartment was also in Elizabeth Beckett's house. Look at this." She handed him an evidence bag with a white handkerchief trimmed in lace in it. "It's exactly like the one we found in David's apartment. You assumed at that point that it was Jordan's."

"Where did you find this," asked Grayson. "It was on the floor of Elizabeth Beckett's closet," Vicki said. "The carpet was depressed a little there like someone was hiding there, waiting." Grayson took the bag back over to his desk and examined the handkerchief under the light. Victoria was right from what he could see. This was the exact type of handkerchief that was found in David's apartment, and at that time, he had assumed it belonged to Jordan. He would have bet money on it. Now he wished he had never said that. The more he thought about it, he was certain that it was the same because he remembered Jordan refusing his handkerchief at the scene and taking one exactly like this from her purse to wipe her eyes. But in truth, he was also more than certain that these handkerchiefs were sold in a boutique where numerous people have shopped, including Elizabeth Beckett.

"So, you mean to tell me that you think that Jordan killed Elizabeth Beckett? Is that what you're saying," asked Grayson trying not to sound angry. "Look, Gray," started Victoria, "I'm not saying that. I'm just going with the evidence, and the evidence proves that she was in both these places, and she is involved with both these people. Nothing says that she killed either of them. I just think that there is something your girlfriend isn't saying. That's all."

"Did the idea occur to you that this could be Elizabeth Beckett's handkerchief? Did you take prints from it? Did you check to see if there were any others among her belongings in her room? I'm certain all the rich women from across the lake have these," he said adamantly. "Whoa, Gray, slow down," said Victoria. "I just said it seemed to be the same handkerchief. No one said it had to be Jordan Chandler's. The evidence is just pointing that way. No, I didn't print it or rummage through a dead woman's belongings to see if more were in her bedroom. Why are you so defensive? Did you fuck her?"

"Really, Vicki? Really? Is that all you think I have on my mind when we have two unsolved murders on our desks," he said, slamming his hand down on his desk. "No, I didn't fuck her. That is unprofessional. She is a suspect, and it's not worth losing my badge over."

"You two, keep it down, we're trying to hear the television. They're doing a special news break," said Andrew from the far corner. Grayson and Victoria stopped their arguing and moved closer to the television. Something had happened, something bad.

"This just in," said the announcer on the screen. "There has been an accident involving millionaire Marcus Beckett, and we will now join Pamela Shaw at the scene." "Yes, Marv, it is a terrible sight," said Pamela. "I'm standing here on the side of S. Hillcrest Road, where it seems Marcus Beckett's limousine has run off the road into a nearby wooded area. The car hit a tree and exploded on impact. From what the coroner has said the vehicle went off sometime during yesterday afternoon. It was just spotted by a group of hikers who were traveling a trail near the crash site. I am sorry to report there were no survivors. Pamela Shaw, live for Channel 22 News." "Well, you heard it here first," said Marv, "millionaire Marcus Beckett dead at the age of 63." The television screen resumed its previous program already in progress.

"Well, that explains why no one had heard from him. He's been dead since yesterday," said Vicki. "Do you think it was a setup. A way to kill them both."

"I don't think so," Grayson said. "From what you stated, the staff said the Becketts had one of their usual blow-ups before Marcus left, but this time he was the one that came out smiling. I don't think a man who had just regained control of his life was thinking about getting killed. Besides, according to you, your guy couldn't kill one person, so I doubt he was a mastermind that planned and pulled off two murders within hours of each other."

"It's kind of sad," said Victoria. "From what I have heard about him, Marcus Beckett was a real nice man. He was very generous and kind, nothing like his wife. But there is a good side to it." "Good side," asked Grayson. "A husband and wife die within hours of each other, how is there a good side of it." "Now, no one has to suffer the loss," said Vicki. "They don't have any children, so no one will have to suffer the loss, not even each other. Neither knew the other had died." Grayson gave it a thought. He guessed when you looked at it that way, Victoria was right.

"And Gray, not to be a bitch, but Marcus makes the third person involved with Jordan. And you never said you didn't want to fuck her, you just said you hadn't because it was unprofessional. You need to get some.

73

I'm game if you are," she said with a smile. Grayson smiled back. He wasn't sure how to comment. "Hmmmm, I take it that's a no," she said. "You do understand that this just motivates me more, right?" Grayson laughed. "Gray, I love it when you laugh," said Victoria. "I'm a very patient and persistent person. I will never give up on you. That is not an option. You were made for me." Grayson just shook his head. "You are so crazy, Victoria. I tell you what, keep trying. I feel my resistance slipping every day." "I know," she said. "And you will be a better man for it." They both laughed while Andrew gave them a dirty look. He hated not being in the loop. He sat right next to them, but he just wasn't a friendly person. They didn't care to talk to him.

"Well, I have to get out of here," said Grayson. "Where are you off to," she asked. "I have some people I have to talk to. Murders don't solve themselves." "Ain't that the truth," she said, grabbing her coat as well. "I guess I'll head back over to the Beckett estate and see what I can dig up. I may have better results with it just being me. People tend to clam up amid the circus." "That's true," said Grayson.

"You wanna meet for coffee later?"

"I thought you hated coffee," she said. "I do, but with the way everything is turning out, I may need it. I feel a lot of long nights ahead of me." "Sure, we can meet up later, just give me a ring," said Vicki. "Gray, if you ever feel like losing yourself in a long night, we can start tonight." "You never quit, do you," he asked. "Never," she replied as they went in opposite directions out the door. Grayson needed to see Jordan. Too many things were happening, and them being coincidental was spreading thin. He needed some more answers from her. That was the truth. Victoria backed down, but she was no fool. She knew how to follow a lead, and she would do that because she was good at her job. She wouldn't want to hurt Grayson, and he was sure of that, but she would do her job just as he would do if the tables were turned.

Jordan walked around her kitchen, coffee cup in hand. She knew she was going into the office today, she just didn't know when. Her head ached a little due to her celebration totties she had the evening before. Normally the hangover would feel much worse, but today the pain was mild. Maybe the ice cream dulled it, she thought to herself. She reached over on the bar and grabbed the remote to see if everyone was still talking about Lizzie. She flipped on her television before settling herself atop one of the stools. Her coffee cup shattered onto the floor. She couldn't believe what she was hearing. Marcus Beckett was dead. MARCUS!! DEAD!! She couldn't believe it. That couldn't possibly be true. Marcus was good and kind. Hadn't he suffered enough in his life? Why did he have to die? She put her hands over her eyes. She could feel the tears forming. She hated when she cried. James hated it even more. He said it disgusted him to no avail. Crying was for babies, which she definitely was not. She looked over at the variety of bottles on the bar. She started to grab one but changed her mind. She would be needed at work today more than ever now. The press would be there, and there would be statements to make. She wasn't ready for all that. She knew that she would have had to present herself as a friend and confidant to Marcus in the eye of the storm. The media would love that, but not this. Now she was going to have to stand there in the wake of all of this with them scrutinizing her every move. Why did you have to go and die on me, Marcus? I was so not ready, she thought to herself.

Jordan didn't even bother cleaning up her coffee on the tile floor. She knew Selina would find it when she got there. She left the kitchen, walking like a zombie. She had to figure out how to play this. She really didn't have to worry about the sympathy part. She was genuinely hurt by Marcus's death. She hated to know that he had gone so violently, accident or not. She hoped that he had died instantly and not suffered. She thought of how he patted her hand in comfort the last time she saw him. He had really cared about her, and despite how she felt about his viper of a wife, she cared about him too. She was shaken from her thoughts by the ringing of her telephone.

"Hello," she said. "Good morning, Jordan, it's me, Gregory Allington." Jordan felt her eyes rolling back into her head, uncontrollably. "Good morning, Mr. Allington," she said into the receiver. "What is it?" "Please call me Greg," he said. "Mr. Allington's my father. I'm calling because I'm certain by now you have heard about the tragedy that has happened concerning the Becketts. I'm sure you are aware of what that means."

"What what means, Gregory," she asked, feigning innocence. She knew exactly what it meant. It was all hers now. The whole company, everything belonged to her. "The company," he continued. "It reverts back to you. It's yours one hundred percent." "Oh," she said. "I'm sorry, Greg, I just hadn't had a chance to think about it. I have only learned about Marcus and Elizabeth since I got up this morning. It's terrible and terribly strange all at once. No one would have ever imagined that there would be two incidents like this. I don't know which is worse."

"I understand," he said. "I just wanted you to know that I would be at your office with some papers for you to sign next week. I could come sooner if you would like." Again, the younger Allington was too eager. She wondered exactly what was in it for him. He seemed very unconcerned about her feelings. It was as if he knew she really didn't care for them. He would be wrong as far as Marcus was concerned. He was tactless at best. "Next week is fine, Greg. I wouldn't be able to concentrate on those matters right now anyway," she said into the receiver.

"I see. Everyone needs their time to mourn," he replied. "I will wait until then. And Jordan, if I may call you Jordan, if you need a shoulder to cry on or someone to talk to, please feel free to call me." Jordan frowned. She knew what he was getting at, but she wasn't interested. He was definitely not her type. "I'll keep that in mind, Greg," she said. "Thank you." She could feel his sick smile through the phone. Just when he began to continue talking, she hung up. She would just pretend she didn't hear him if he brought it up next week.

Jordan passed through the living room to head up the stairs when she just happened to glance a form through the glass of her front door. It was a woman. The doorbell rang as soon as she headed back in that direction. "Yes," she said, opening the door. She hated it when Selina came in later than normal. She really didn't look the part answering her door in a bathroom. The woman at the door was taller than her with a slim figure. She had black hair and brown doe eyes. "May I help you," Jordan asked. "I'm Investigator Victoria Evans. I'm looking for Ms. Jordan Chandler," she said. "I'm Jordan Chandler, Investigator. How can I help you?"

Victoria gave her an up and down once over. She didn't see anything special about her. She would have to get with Grayson about his choices in women. She didn't hide her look of disapproval from Jordan. "I just have a few questions for you," said Victoria. "Please sit down," Jordan said, motioning her hand towards the sofa. "Can I offer you some coffee? Is this about David? I thought Grayson was handling his case." Victoria shot her a sideways glance. "Investigator Jeffcoat is handling that case, but we are partners. Besides, this has nothing to do with your fiancé's case. I'm here about Elizabeth Beckett." Jordan tried not to look shocked. Why would she be here about Lizzie? Lamar said he swept everything. "I just heard about what happened to her this morning," said Jordan trying not to appear nervous. "It was terrible. I hope they find who did it," she said, sitting in a chair opposite Victoria. "Yes, I hope we do too. We are just going around speaking with people who knew her so that we can get a feel for what kind of person she was," said Victoria. "Ms. Chandler, what did you think of Mrs. Beckett?"

"She seemed nice. She was a very old friend of my family," Jordan said, making sure not to give away anything. "We heard that you and she had just recently become business partners via your father's will," said Vicki. "Her husband Marcus and I had become partners. She was included as his spouse. Terrible thing that has happened to Marcus as well. I just can't believe it," Jordan said. "That is what everyone is saying," said Victoria. "Both of them out of the way just like that." Victoria looked directly at Jordan when she made that statement. Jordan didn't flinch. She knew she was being baited. "Marcus was a good man. He will be missed. He was always like an uncle to me," she replied. "Investigator Evans, I hate to rush you, but I must get ready for work. I'm sure it's a circus there already. Do you have any more questions?" "No, that will do for now," said Victoria standing. "If I have any more, I'll be sure to get in touch with you." Jordan nodded as she led Victoria towards the door. "Please feel free to contact me," she said, opening the door. "I will do that," said Victoria. "Have a good day, Ms. Chandler or at least the best one you can have under the circumstances." Jordan watched Victoria walk down the stairs and closed the door behind her.

Jordan stood with her back against the door. She didn't like Victoria Evans. She didn't like her snooping around her home. She didn't like being asked questions, and she definitely didn't like the way she said that she and Grayson were "partners." There was something about her that rubbed her the wrong way. She seemed like she thought she had it figured out. Jordan thought for sure she was going to tell her not to leave town. She didn't know it, but Investigator Victoria Evans had earned herself a spot on her list, and that was somewhere she didn't want to be. She would have to think of something creative for her. Jordan wondered if Grayson knew she was going to pay her a visit. She would be sure to ask him the next time they spoke. She headed upstairs to get ready for her day. It would be a busy one, indeed.

Grayson sat across the street from J. Chandler Enterprises. No one even noticed him, not that he had expected them to. He had been there for about an hour, and the front entrance was bombarded with reporters. He felt sorry for Jordan. It was like she kept getting knocked down every time she got back up. He hadn't seen her come into work this morning, not that she would take the front entrance. He was sure that she knew they would be here. He was getting a weird feeling in his gut about her, and he didn't like weird feelings. It was as if people were dropping like flies around her. He hoped that she wouldn't be next. The only death so far that seemed to be an act of God was her father's. He hoped that remained true. He admired her strength. Even in the midst of what was going on around her, she seemed to be holding it together. Well, for the most part, he thought as he remembered her drinking. He was going to have to ask her some more questions. That was going to be a bittersweet moment. He wanted to see her again, but he didn't want to upset her any more than she already was. He didn't want to see her cry again. He would be lying if he said it didn't affect him. It did. He was able to control himself when she kissed him the last time, he wasn't sure he would be able to if it happened again.

His phone rang. "Yeah, Vicki, what's up," he said. "We need to talk," she said. "About what? What's going on?"

"I paid your girlfriend a visit this morning," replied Victoria. "You did what," Grayson asked. "I went to question her about Mrs. Beckett. She didn't like her. Her mouth didn't say so, but everything else did," she said.

"Why would you do that, Vicki," Grayson asked. "She isn't even involved in your case."

"I know, but she's hiding something Gray. I don't know what it is, but she's not telling us everything."

"And now she probably won't thanks to you," he snapped. "I told you I had this under control." "Look, Gray, I know what you said, and I wasn't trying to step on your toes," she continued, "but I think you are getting a little caught up with her. She even referred to you by your first name, like you all were friends. I know you know how to do your job. I was just helping out."

"No, you weren't. You were butting in like you do," he said. "Victoria, I don't need a baby sitter. You stick to your cases and leave me to mine. Do you understand me?" There was a bit of uncomfortable silence on the phone. "Victoria," he said.

"I'm here," she replied. "I understand."

"GOOD," he said as he hit end. Where does she get off? Victoria is just too much at times. Maybe he had been a bit rough on her, but she deserved it. She couldn't keep going off halfcocked like that just because she's trying to prove a point. He would explain how he felt about it later and apologize. Maybe. Grayson returned his attention to the other side of the street just in time to see a curly bun over the collar of a gray suit disappear into the media mob.

Twelve

Jordan stood at her desk and watched all the people in motion around her. There were PR personnel, lawyers, investors, board members and, of course, the media clamoring outside to just get one word with her. They needed her comments. She didn't think so, but then again, they may be interested in what she had to say. Truthfully, she didn't know what she had to say yet. It was all being written by one of the spin doctors right now. She would have been perfectly fine with just giving her condolences and tearing up in front of the camera. That was thoughtful. That was human. Her people, however, wanted her to give one of these statements in which she carried on about the loss of Marcus and Elizabeth and how society was better just by having them in it. That, however, was partially true. In Marcus's case, yes. Lizzie, however, could have gone down in the pits long ago. It would have been nobody's loss. "Ms. Chandler," said Susan, one of her writers. She really liked Susan. She had the kind of face that screamed milk and cookies. "Ms. Chandler, if you would take a look at this and tell me what you think. We can revise it a bit if you would like, but the board thinks this is the best statement to give." Jordan gave it a quick once over. It contained all of the regular bits. In parentheses at the bottom, it said, "show sadness and dismay." Really, dismay, she thought to herself. She really wanted to just tear it up right in front of them. She could go out there and give them a statement they would be playing for the next year or so. But she couldn't. Being who she was would not allow it. It would not allow her to genuinely grieve for her lost father figure. She had to mourn him equally with a person she hated. They had to be equals, at least in public. She looked up from the paper and handed it back to Susan. "That will be fine," she said, turning her back on the crowd. "Ms. Chandler," Susan said again. "I hate to bother you, but you need to choose one network to give your statement to." Jordan turned back around and thought about it. "I'll give it to Craig Phipps, of Channel 11," she said. Craig was once her lover, and her statement would help him out a lot. Plus, she had a way to unnerve him when he was working. That would bring her a little joy today.

"Okay," Susan said, nodding as she moved over to the crowd to convey Jordan's wishes.

"Everybody, I need a minute," Jordan said over the chatty crowd. Everyone ceased talking and cleared her office immediately.

Jordan sat back in her chair and spun around so that she could see the window. Everything looked small from where she was. Maybe that was her problem. She felt small. No matter how much power she got, she still felt small. Invisible sometimes. She walked over to the window and looked down. I would be dead in seconds, she thought to herself. But where would the fun lie in that? Who would care anyway? Just another dead, rich whore. That's what the headlines would read. She wouldn't go out like that. She would go out a legend, one way or the other. "Jordan, they're ready for you now," said Rebecca. Jordan threw up her hand in acknowledgment. She turned around and smoothed down the front of her jacket and headed for the foyer. She was joined by four men of various sizes as she entered the elevator to head downstairs to face the music.

Grayson Jeffcoat decided to stand outside of his truck to get a better view of what was going on as he watched the crowd become alive as if preparing for someone's arrival. He watched a man come out and motion for a reporter to move forward and set his cameraman up on the side. After this was done, he saw Jordan being ushered to a makeshift platform in the middle of the crowd. All he could really hear at first were the cameras snapping and reporters throwing questions at her. She, however, was focusing her attention on the reporter that had been moved to the right. She nodded and gave a brief smile. She looked a little pale like she didn't feel well. He imagined she didn't. She finished her statement and stepped back. An older gentleman with gray hair took a step on to the platform and began speaking. Jordan just stood behind and watched. She watched everything— the crowd, the man in front of her, even the street. He looked up, and just for a second, their eyes met. Her lips parted as if she wanted to say something. She didn't. The man finished his speech and stepped down. He placed his hand at the small of Jordan's back and guided her inside the building. For some reason, Grayson didn't like him placing his hand there.

He didn't like it one bit. He wondered what Jordan had wanted to tell him. Her eyes were calling to him, but what could he do. He was stuck. She is a suspect, he kept telling himself. You can't do this.

The day seemed to drag for Jordan. It had been hours since she had given her statement, and the phones just kept ringing off the hooks. It was like they weren't getting answered fast enough. Jordan hated the sound they made. She just wanted some peace and quiet, that's all. She didn't think that was too much to ask for. She would have loved to just be able to go home, but it seemed like the wrong thing to do. All it would take was one phone call to the newspapers that her business was having issues and she had darted out the back door like a coward. She didn't need that. It wasn't that there were problems. It was just the fact that she would now be taking full control of her father's business—her business. Some board members were okay with it, some others had problems. She couldn't understand why. This business was the one thing she knew. It was like it had been a father to her. Whenever James had meetings or was just tired of her, he would drop her off in various offices, and she did what most kids do. She listened. She listened, and she learned so much. She could even rival James, and in some areas like technology, she had surpassed him.

She thought about seeing Grayson standing across the street. Why was he there? Was he spying on her? Probably, she thought. He said he was going to call today. He hadn't yet. Maybe he felt sorry for her. He could see her face. He saw her pain. That was what had made him back off. She was sure of it. He looked delicious. She couldn't deny it. Leaning against his truck, arms folded across his massive chest and looking as sexy as sin. She couldn't deny the draw that she had to him. He gave her that smile. The one where he cocked his head a little to the right and smiled all the way into his dimple. Too sexy. She had hoped that she would have had a chance to sample him by now. But everything had happened so quickly—the whole Marcus fiasco. No one saw that coming. Now everyone is picking up the pieces. He is hard to replace. Replace is not the word since he never really got started. Jordan's head began to hurt. She knew what could cure that. A bottle of vodka and her bed. She knew that would do it or maybe a night with Grayson Jeffcoat. That made her smile. She was sure that would help her out more than the vodka. She didn't feel like she wanted to get drunk. She only did that when she wanted to avoid problems or get over things. She wasn't really in that kind of mood. She was actually feeling good, other than the loss of Marcus. Maybe she would do something fun tonight—something just for her.

The day had dragged on for Grayson as well. After leaving J. Chandler Enterprises, he had pretty much just driven around. He never called Victoria for coffee. He was still mad at her. She had actually called three times since. He had sent her to voicemail, which was something he had never done before. This wasn't the first time he had been angry with her, but it was the angriest he had ever been with her. He was sure she knew it. He was never disagreeable with her, and even in his maddest, he had never not answered her calls. His voicemail icon was lit up on his phone. He was certain that she had left him some choice messages. Grayson laughed to himself. Victoria had a way with words, especially bad ones. Hopefully, she would allow him to smooth it over with her tomorrow, or maybe she was going to make him suffer it out. He guessed he would have to wait and see. He kept allowing his mind to drift back to Jordan. Why was he so concerned about her? He knew why. It was because he was a decent guy, and she needed help. She was his new damsel in distress. That made him laugh, Jordan Chandler was hardly a damsel in distress. She had everything anyone would want, but he still couldn't help but see the loneliness in her eyes. He guessed it was true, money couldn't buy happiness. At least it didn't for her.

Victoria did give him a great idea in her error in judgment. Maybe he could go and do a little investigating on his own out at the Beckett estate. Sure, he had told Vicki to stick to her cases, and he would do the same, but she had already breached the contract by going over to Jordan's. Grayson turned his radio up a notch. Bon Jovi was howling, "You give love a bad name," and he sped up to the tempo heading out to the Beckett estate. Maybe someone there would know something to help both he and Victoria out. They may also know something to clear or convict Jordan. His hopes rested on the former.

Victoria sat at her desk. That was the third time she had called Grayson. She hoped everything was okay with him. He always answered her calls. She felt kind of bad. She wasn't feeling all that concerned when she cursed him out on the first two messages. She knew he would forgive her. He always did. He had a good sense of humor. That was one of the things she liked about him—one of the many things. Victoria had to admit to herself, she had really fallen for Grayson. He never noticed, though. He felt that she was always teasing in fun. She was, but as the old saying goes, there's truth in jest. She would like nothing better than to be the girl he smiled at in that way. But he only saw her as a friend. Was that her problem? Was she jealous of Jordan Chandler? Victoria couldn't believe that. She was not the type of woman who compared herself to other women. She always held her own. She knew she was better than average looking, funny and intelligent. She was also taller than a lot of men she met, had a base sense of humor and was known to have a temper. Carrying a gun didn't help much, either. But with Gray, she didn't have to worry about that. He loved all of that about her. He always said, "Vicki, don't change a thing," or "Be careful, Vicki. I wouldn't want anything to happen to my girl." His girl, she said to herself. But he didn't mean it like that. He meant it more of a guy friend sort of way. That hurt more than outright rejection. Maybe she would be able to convince him one day. That was if he ever spoke to her again.

Victoria didn't feel that she was on some kind of unspoken vendetta against Jordan; it was just that things kept happening, and she was the key factor in all of them. If Grayson wasn't caught up in the idea of fucking her brains out, he could see that. He would see that. He was a great investigator. He always caught the little things that other people didn't see. But not this time. This time he wasn't reading any of the signs. She knew that she would have to do it, at least until he got his dick wet or his head out of the clouds. She would only consider the first one if she was doing the wetting. She decided to have forensics run some tests on the handkerchiefs. Grayson did say that they did make more than one or, in this case, two, but she needed to know for herself. She could prove that her theory had legs and that she just wasn't some covetous nut job. Even though that was exactly what she was.

Grayson pulled up to the Beckett estate, and it seemed very quiet. He could see a few lights on in a couple of windows, but it didn't seem like a lot was going on. It especially didn't seem like a place that was preparing to mourn its employers. He knocked on the door. "Yes, coming," a female voice said from the other side. The door opened, and a small woman of around forty years old stood. She was dressed in a gray maid's uniform, complete with headdress and apron. "How may I help you," she asked. "I'm Investigator Jeffcoat. I just have a few questions regarding Mr. and Mrs. Beckett," he said. "Another one," she said, walking furiously through the foyer throwing up her hands. "Don't mind her," said another voice which belonged to a maid heading down the stairwell to his right. "Maria doesn't like police. She finds them to be very troubling. I'm Carly," she said. "Investigator Jeffcoat," Grayson said, extending his hand to her. "So, I've heard," she said.

"Carly, I have a few questions about your employers if you don't mind," he said. "No, I don't mind," she replied. "What is it that you wish to know?" "Well, for starters," he said, looking around the room, "where is everyone? It doesn't look as if you are preparing to memorialize the Becketts."

"We're not," said Carly. "There is no one to memorialize." "What do you mean by that," he asked. "Well, Mr. Beckett went to pieces. All that we have is here," she said, pointing to the urn on a table nearest the door. "What about Mrs. Beckett," he asked. "There won't be a service for her either," said Carly. "Mrs. Beckett's sister came and took her body back to their family home. She said since Mr. Marcus was gone, there was no reason for her sister to stay here." Grayson gave her a dismayed look but made no comment. "So, what is going to happen to the estate," Grayson asked. "Oh, it's going to charity," said Carly. "Mr. Marcus had a will which left everything he had to charity. He knew Mrs. Elizabeth was a spendthrift, and he had worked very hard for his money," she said. "She had been waiting for Mr. Marcus to die for a long time now." "Who was," asked Grayson, making notes as she spoke. "Mrs. Elizabeth," said Carly. "She had big plans for this money. She had big, big plans."

"What kind of plans," Grayson asked. "I'm not at liberty to say, sir. You know speaking ill of the dead." Grayson just looked at her and nodded. "Tell me, Carly," Grayson said. "Did Mrs. Beckett have a lot of visitors?" Carly dropped her eyes to the floor. He knew what that meant. It was obvious that Elizabeth Beckett had many male visitors. It didn't matter if Carly told him so or not. He knew. "Is there any more information you would like to give Carly," he asked softly. "Do you know who made the call about Mrs. Beckett? Do you have any idea who that could be," he asked. Carly shook her head. "No one knows, it's like there was a ghost. To my knowledge, no one came in or out of the room, but no one owned up to making the call. "I see," said Grayson. "Thank you again, do you mind if I look around a bit," he said. Carly shrugged her shoulders. "Just don't destroy anything." Grayson nodded in compliance as he headed up the stairs.

Once he got to Elizabeth Beckett's room, everything looked immaculate. If there had been any type of residual evidence left behind, it had been thoroughly cleaned. The maids here took pride in their service and made certain that everywhere was picture perfect. The bed was made as if Marcus and Elizabeth were out on the town and would be crashing there later tonight. Grayson decided to venture over to the closet since that was where Victoria said she had found the handkerchief. It was huge, almost as big as the room itself. Grayson didn't know where to begin. There were many places to hide things. He would just have to check them all. He began with the clothes. He checked all the pockets to see if the perp had hidden something there. He found nothing. He looked in the shoe boxes, the purses, the accessory bags…nothing. He began to look in the carpet for hair fibers and on the clothes again. He found mostly black hair, which he knew belonged to Elizabeth. There were some short brown hairs that he assumed belonged to Marcus. Before he left the closet, he found more hair ranging from blonde to red. He assumed they were from the many maids. He didn't feel that it was necessary to check every piece, so he decided he would take the ones that he thought were strange. The curly hairs were from the floor, and the red ones were on a coat sleeve. He dropped both of them in sample bags he kept in his jacket. All of the maids he saw had dark hair, that wasn't to say they didn't have a blonde or redheaded maid, but he couldn't ask without the whole staff getting suspicious. They assumed the cops had their man, and he didn't need to give them any reason not to think so.

He left the closet and searched under the bed on the side where Elizabeth was found. He didn't see anything unfamiliar. A pair of bedroom slippers was pushed under that side and some kind of black box. Grayson reached underneath and pulled out the box. It wasn't locked. It was filled with pictures. The pictures were of Elizabeth and numerous men. Sometimes there was more than one man in the photograph. She was keeping a photographic record of her trysts. Why would she do that, he thought. The more he looked at the pictures, he saw that she wasn't posing or holding the camera. These pictures were taken with surveillance equipment. Marcus was taking these pictures. He knew everything she did, and she wasn't aware. He was planning to reveal it. This is why he kept the photos. He was going to let her know that he knew about her secret meetings. This led to a lot of questions. Did she figure it out? Did she plot to kill Marcus to keep his fortune? There was no way he was giving her anything with all this evidence. He continued flipping through the box, looking at the faces of the men to see if he recognized any of them. To his dismay, he did. There was the mayor giving her a piggyback ride and two senators lying in bed smoking cigars with her in between them. He had voted for the one on the right. He had almost reached the bottom of the box when he saw a pair of familiar sable eyes staring up at him. This was Jordan's father. He was sure of it. Victoria and the gossip mongers were right. He was having an affair with her. Poor Jordan. He wondered if she knew.

Grayson closed the box and slid it back under the bed. He would have to find a way to come back and get it. He most definitely couldn't take it downstairs with him. His mind turned to something else. All of the pictures were taken in this room. This meant there was surveillance equipment here, or there was at one time. Grayson began looking in places he felt someone could hide a camera. He looked in the headboard, the window sill, the bedpost, the armoire across from the bed, but he didn't see anything. Wherever they were, they had to be in the proximity of the bed from the angles on the photos. He would have to have someone come back in and do a sweep. If the equipment was still here and in operation when the murder took place, they would have their murderer. That's all the evidence they would need.

Grayson took a look at Elizabeth's vanity table. It was loaded with perfumes and creams. He saw a tissue that had a smear of red lipstick on it next to the silver tray that held her wedding ring. Well, he could say her staff was honest. If not, that ring would have been long gone, but it remained there as if she had just taken it off. Before he could take a step into the bathroom, he heard the sound of someone clearing their throat. It was Carly. "Are you done," she asked. "I have to get back to work before Maria breaks my neck. She doesn't want you here." "Yeah. I'm done," he replied. Carly led the way to the bedroom door.

"Carly, were you here the day Mrs. Beckett was killed?" he asked. "Yes, but I arrived right before the police did. She was already dead," she replied. "Everyone was hysterical, especially Derrick. He kept screaming what had he done, what had he done."

"You heard him say that," asked Grayson. "Are you sure?"

"Sure, I'm sure," she replied. "Of course, he changed his tune by the time your guys got here, but that's what he said." "Thanks, Carly, you've been a great help," he said, grabbing her by the shoulders before running down the stairs. Grayson closed the door as quiet as possible. He didn't want to give Carly away after she had been so kind. Carly watched as Grayson closed the door, and she smiled. She almost felt bad for lying to him. He seemed to be a nice man, for a cop anyway. That was the easiest ten thousand dollars she had ever made. Lamar told her it would be easy. He bought it all. She had given him just enough to keep them off of Jordan's scent. Lamar was always looking out for her, and she would thank him energetically for it later. She just hoped it worked.

Thirteen

When Grayson got back to his car, he felt relieved. He knew that Jordan wasn't a killer. He didn't understand why he even allowed what Victoria said to him stick in his head. She had a way of getting under his skin, he had to admit that. Carly said Derrick confessed. She was adamant about it enough so that he knew if he subpoenaed her to court, she would testify. That cleared Jordan for sure, cleared her for this murder. He knew he should be concentrating on David Anderson's case. The man was in the ground, and they were really no farther along than they were days after it happened. He had already found a great many things that would lead to more questions in this case. He would have to get with Victoria to have her get a warrant to retrieve the box and check for surveillance equipment and tapes before the estate was seized by charity and sold off for the money. She wouldn't be happy that he had gone behind his back, but she had done the same. They would work it out. They always did. But for now, he was happy. He had a confession, even though it was hearsay. He would have to lean on Derrick a little more tomorrow if he hadn't bonded out. He looked at his watch. It was going on eight o'clock. He hadn't called Jordan like he promised. She had had a rough day. A rough month was more like it. He wouldn't call her now. She probably wanted to be left alone or maybe not. He would think about that as he drove back into the city.

"Teddy, do you have anything yet," said Victoria as she paced the lab floor. "Give me a second Vicki, will you? You can't just bring me something and expect me to say hocus pocus and give you a result," he replied. "These things take time." "I know," she responded. "I'm just antsy. I really need to find this out."

"Which case is this on?" Teddy asked. "It's actually two, one of mine and one of Gray's," said Vicki. "Oh, I see," he said. "Gray doesn't know about this, does he? That's why you're in a rush to finish before he finds out. I swear, Victoria, you are always pushing his buttons, and one day, he's going to push back. I don't want to be around when that happens." Victoria gave him a smirk and sat in the chair behind Teddy's desk. Theodore Hollister was one of the best forensic scientists around. He stood at a table across from her, his blond head bent. He didn't look much like a scientist. He looked more like a European spy, very Bond-esque. Victoria was thankful for his help, but she really shouldn't have involved Teddy in her mess. She knew he would do it for her because he had a crush on her. She hated to play on that, but she did, from time to time, if it could get her evidence rushed through.

"Don't worry about Gray, I'll do that. You just finish up what you're doing," she said. "Fine," Teddy replied. "But when he comes shooting darts out of those gray eyes of his, I'm sending him in your direction." Victoria laughed. "Anyway, you were right about this, Victoria. These handkerchiefs belong to the same person. We just don't know who that person is. I pulled a fingerprint off of the backs of both. The fingerprint matched, but it didn't match anyone in the system. So that's your dilemma," said Teddy.

"Well, at least that's a start," she replied. "Maybe now he won't think I'm completely crazy." "You know who these belong to," he asked. "I have an idea, but nothing is set in concrete. I have some more digging to do," replied Victoria. "Is there any way you can get a personal item from the person you think this belongs to," asked Teddy. "If you can get me something with their fingerprints on it, I can match it to the ones I have and give you your suspect. This person is a suspect, right?" "Sort of," replied Victoria. "I'll see what I can do." Victoria took the bagged handkerchiefs from Teddy to put back on Gray's desk. She didn't want him to know she did even more meddling. "Hey, Vicki, how about joining me for a drink tomorrow night," Teddy said, catching her off guard. "I don't know, Teddy," she said. "I need to gather some more evidence. You know homicide. Never a dull moment." "Sure. I know how it is," Teddy said. "I know you're still stuck on him, Vicki, but when you realize that it's not going to happen, hopefully, I'll still be around to help you pick up the pieces. Gray's a nice guy, but he doesn't see you in that way. You don't know what you're missing out on pining over him." Victoria smiled at

Teddy. He was right and cute in his honesty. She knew that Gray didn't see her that way, but she couldn't bring herself to give up hope, not yet. "I hope you're still around too, Teddy. If I finish early tomorrow, we can have that drink. I'll stop by when I'm done." Teddy gave her a grin. "A pity drink, or is it a guilt drink because I did this for you, and I won't tell Gray? Either way, I'll take it," he said. "I won't leave until I hear from you." "Ok, I'll see you tomorrow, Ted and thanks for everything," said Victoria as she left through the swinging doors.

Grayson found himself in front of Jordan's house. He wasn't sure how he got there. Well, he knew how he got there, but that wasn't really his intent. He had thought about the day she had and felt she may have needed a friend. He wasn't her friend and he kept telling himself. But he wanted to be. He felt like he was. He should have just called. What if she wasn't home? What if she was and told him to get lost? He hadn't thought this through. He should just drive off. He didn't. He parked his truck across the street and walked up to the door. He rang the doorbell and, in that instant, hoped that she didn't answer.

Jordan heard the doorbell. She looked at the clock. It was a quarter to nine. Who would be visiting her at this time of night? She looked down at her clothes. She was wearing a pair of shorts from her college volleyball team and a t-shirt. She heard the bell ring once more and decided to get up. Whoever it was would just have to accept her like this. She only hoped it wasn't the paparazzi.

Grayson stood at her door and waited. If she didn't come out in the next minute, he was leaving. It was stupid to come here, to begin with. He heard her footsteps coming down the stairs just as he was turning his back. Jordan looked through her peephole and was shocked at what she saw. There was Grayson Jeffcoat at her front door. He didn't look like he was on official business. He was wearing a black tee that was molded to his powerful frame, worn jeans and what looked like motorcycle boots. He looked hot. Jordan had to catch herself. She looked a hot mess. She didn't want him to see her like this, but she didn't want him to leave either. She needed to find out what he wanted or, better yet, what he knew.

"Who's there," she asked even though she knew. "Hi, it's me, Grayson. Investigator Jeffcoat," he said. Jordan took a deep breath and opened the door. "Hi, Grayson," she said, looking down at her feet. "Hi, Jordan," he said. "I'm sorry to interrupt your evening. I told you I was going to give you a call and I didn't. I wanted to tell you about Elizabeth Beckett, and then before I could, the whole thing happened with Marcus, and I never got around to it. I guess I just wanted to check on you. I know today has been hard for you. Again, I'm sorry to disturb you. I'll let you get back to what you were doing." And with that, he turned to walk away.

"Grayson," she said, "you don't have to leave. You can come in if you would like." He felt a weight lift off of his chest. "Are you sure," he asked. "Because I can go. I'm not here in any official capacity. I thought you might have just needed a friend." Jordan smiled, and then he gave her that smile, the sexy one. What could she say after that? "Are we friends, Grayson," she asked, testing the waters. "We are," he replied even though he knew he was playing with fire. If the wrong people got wind of this, he would be done for. "Good, because I could really use one," said Jordan. "Won't you come in," she said, stepping to the side to let him in.

Jordan's living room seemed enormous. She had a huge sofa in the middle of the floor with a recliner off to the left side. There was a fireplace and a few end tables. It was kind of eccentric, but elegant at the same time. Grayson had to admit he kind of liked it. "Pardon my outfit. I was just hanging out upstairs. I really wasn't expecting anyone." Grayson gave her a once over. She was wearing short shorts, a tee, and flip flops. Her hair was full, in a halo of curls, some hanging just below her shoulders. She was wearing pink toenail polish. What was there to pardon? Everything looked good to him. "No, you're fine. I mean, you look fine. I could say the same about my outfit." "You look fine too," she said. "Please sit down." She gestured to the sofa. Grayson took a seat at the very end of the couch. Jordan sat down beside him. There was an awkward silence. Neither of them was sure what to say.

"Sorry about your day," Grayson started. "I know it's been a tough one. You've had a lot of tough ones here of late." Jordan pulled her legs underneath her on the couch. Very flexible, Grayson thought to himself. "It has been," she said, interrupting his train of thought. "It's been much harder than I imagined. I was somewhat prepared for James's death. He had been training me in one way or another all my life. But David, now Elizabeth and Marcus, it's just been a bad experience all around. I'm tired of speeches, I'm tired of the press, I'm just tired of people altogether."

"I see," said Grayson inching forward. "I'll get going." "I don't mean you, Grayson," she said, putting her hand on his thigh. "I'm happy to see you." That brought a smile to his face, which helped him deflect from the feeling of her hand being on his thigh. It was as if she had read his thoughts and quickly moved it, but not before allowing two of her fingers to move a little bit higher. Grayson sat down quickly before desire reared its ugly head.

"I just thought a little company would do you good. It always works when I'm in the dumps," he said. "I'm sure being a cop has its number of bad days too," she said, scooting a little closer on the couch. Grayson's stomach did a funny flip. She didn't need to come any closer. He could already smell her perfume, and at the angle she was sitting, her neck looked perfect for him to bend into and take a whiff. He couldn't do that. If he leaned into her, so many things would happen. If she didn't reject him, he would be on her taking as many liberties as he could. But that wasn't a good idea at all. "Grayson, did you hear me," she asked. "I'm sorry, what?" he asked. "You have more bad days than good ones," she said. "It seems that way most of the time," he said, getting a leash on his mind. "I understand," she said, scooting a little closer, her hair brushing his shoulder.

"Jordan, I also needed to apologize to you," he said. "Why?" Jordan leaned forward to look into his eyes. "For Victoria. She told me she came by today." She dropped her eyes to her lap. "She did. She actually came by before I left for work this morning. I had just heard about Marcus on the news and was devastated." Grayson looked into her eyes. He knew she wasn't lying. Her pain for Marcus had been real. "She asked a few questions about Elizabeth. She said she is handling that investigation. She also told me she was your partner." Grayson leaned back on to the couch.

"We are partners, but I didn't send her here. She thought that since you were acquainted with Elizabeth Beckett and her husband that maybe you could give her some clues on Elizabeth's character. Since this wasn't a B&E, we are wondering why someone would want to kill her."

"I thought you guys had someone in custody," she said looking towards the door. "His picture has been plastered all over the news. It was a crime of passion, right?" "So, it had seemed, but it just wasn't adding up for me, at least until tonight," he replied.

"Tonight?" she asked. "What's happened tonight?"

"Not much, I just have someone who heard Delgado confess to killing her. I just have to make it stick," he replied. "But enough about my work, that's not why I'm here. How are you, Jordan, really? What can I do to make you feel better?" If this had been anyone other than Grayson Jeffcoat, she would have taken that last statement as innuendo, but she knew that wasn't what he meant. He was genuinely concerned about her. It was actually kind of endearing.

"I'm fine, Grayson. It's just been very trying and very tiring," she said. "I can't get anything done because more things keep popping up. The investors are not happy about the current changes that are taking place. They didn't want me to have the helm of this company. They kept saying I was too young, female and sadly, Black. When they found out that James had snuck Marcus on board, they were pacified. They knew that he would make most of the decisions and then bring them to me for my approval. They knew he had the best head for business and would make only the best decisions for the company. I was going to be more of a figurehead, you know like Queen Elizabeth," she said, making a crown motion over her head. Grayson couldn't help but laugh. She was funny. He liked funny. "So, when they found out that Marcus had perished in this accident, they were back to square one. They were only concerned about damage control and figuring out what their next move was. They didn't even give me time to mourn Marcus. He was like an uncle to me. He and my father had been best friends for a long time until they fell out. But even with that, Marcus remained close to our family. I respected him as a person, not for how much money he was going to bring in for me. They had one concern. What was the company to do now that all the big, strong men were dead and had left a little deer in headlights like myself to run things? They are really pissing me off." Grayson sat up and took notice. From her expression, he had no doubt they were pissing her off. And from the looks of it, that was something they really didn't want to do.

"Well, they will just have to get over it," Grayson said. "It's your company. It's your birthright, your father's legacy. They will get over it." "I'm more like my father's curse," she said. "They all wished he'd had a boy. James wished so too."

"James, I'm lost," Grayson said. "Who is James?"

"Sorry," Jordan said. "James is my father. He never allowed me to call him dad, or daddy or even father, just James." Grayson just stared at her. What kind of parenting was this? He would have had his lips smacked if he would have even said the Hen in Henry. That was totally unacceptable. "What about your mom," Grayson asked. "How did she feel about that?" "My mom died when I was very young, and she was the exact opposite of James," she replied. "I loved my mother, and I took it very hard when she died. I wish she was here now. Things would be so much better."

Grayson leaned over and lifted her chin. "Hey, look at me, things will get better. Trust me, but you have to concentrate on you. You need to take better care of yourself. It's going to all blow over." Jordan looked up into those wonderful blue-grays. "I hope it does for the sake of everyone involved," she said. Grayson stroked the bottom of her chin with his thumb, the little rhythm giving her a warm feeling down to her toes. He had a way with words. She felt comforted already, but there were better ways for her to feel. With any luck, they would come into play soon enough.

Grayson had to catch himself after realizing what he was doing. It was as if she was hypnotizing him with the green in her eyes. He felt something profound for her, and he wanted to comfort her. He didn't like the sad look in her eyes, and from what he had just learned about her parents, he imagined she had been sad for a long time. No one should have to live like that.

"Sorry," he said, drawing back his hand. "I get carried away sometimes." She smiled. "It's okay. I do too, sometimes," she said before placing a light kiss on Grayson's cheek. His mind did a U-turn at that moment. He wasn't sure what to do. His body said, "go with it," but his brain was shouting, "you know better." His body won out. Grayson leaned in and gave Jordan a soft kiss on the lips. She moaned just a little when their mouths touched. That was all the encouragement he needed. He wrapped his arms around her waist and pulled her closer to him and kissed her again, but this time the kiss wasn't as soft. It was long and hard. He sucked on that luscious bottom lip of hers, and she plunged her tongue into his mouth again. This sent his mind reeling. It was even better than the first time. He was afraid to release her because he didn't want this to just be another one of his fantasies.

Jordan broke the kiss only for an instant to settle herself on his lap. The intense look in her eyes told him everything he needed to know. This time she took the lead, biting his lower lip. Her hands eagerly exploring him, running over his shoulders and down his arms. She then ran her palms over his chest, feeling the hard muscle that lay beneath his T-shirt. Grayson could hardly catch his breath. He ran his fingers through her hair, along her jaw, down the sides of her neck. He then moved on to caressing her back before bringing one hand around to touch her stomach, where her shirt had rose. He slowly moved his hand up to cup one of her breasts. It felt perfect in his hand. Jordan released a gasp of delight, and he increased his torture by running his palm over her nipple as it hardened beneath the fabric.

Jordan began pressing her ass down harder on his erection, grinding into him. It was driving him insane. It felt so good, his jeans felt as though they had shrunk two sizes. He prayed his zipper didn't break. She lowered her hand between the two of them and dipped it into the front of her shorts. She took it back out with two of her fingers glistening from her wetness. She put one of them in her mouth and began to slowly suck it with her eyes closed. She looked as if it tasted so good it made Grayson hungry. She then, in turn, put the other finger in his mouth. My god she tasted as good as she looked, he thought to himself. It was like peaches and vanilla cream, and Grayson had to have more.

She slid off of Grayson's lap and onto the floor between his legs. She lifted the bottom of his shirt and began to place kisses all around the bottom of his stomach. She ran her tongue into his belly button, which caused him to almost buck off of the couch. She ran her hands underneath his shirt to feel the soft hair that covered it. While exploring, she pinched both of his nipples, which caused his crotch to tighten even more. Jordan looked down at his erection. She moved her hands up and down the shaft through his jeans. "I can take care of that if you want me to," she said. "It will make us both feel better." Again, there was the protest within him. So far, it was just crossing the line a little; if he did this, there was really no going back. He looked down at her, honeyed eyes shining, beautiful pouty lips parted with a look that said eager to please. He couldn't say no. Only a fool would have said no, and Grayson Jeffcoat was no fool. He nodded his head in agreement and closed his eyes in anticipation.

Jordan smiled up at Grayson. She knew what she was doing. She knew all too well. Without hesitation, she slowly pulled down his zipper. She had to admit she was more than willing. She had thought about it since the first time she saw him, this and so much more. As far as she could see, there were no drawbacks to it. She was getting what she wanted, and so was he. She was also getting a new way to control the situation and control was something she was all about. She was sure that she wouldn't have a problem with this investigation anymore. Grayson's manhood looked just the way she imagined it, hard and thick. It was the perfect size for her. It had a huge mushroom head that she was more than happy to feel at the back of her throat. She lunged forward and devoured the whole shaft. Grayson opened his eyes. They mirrored his shock and disbelief. A beautiful woman was giving him a blow, a beautiful woman that he was interested in. A beautiful woman who was a suspect and a person of interest in two murders, his conscience nagged. At that moment, he didn't care. He could care less about any of it. He drew in his breath. Right now, it wouldn't've mattered if she killed fifty people. "You feel so good," he said, his breathing increasing. Jordan didn't say anything. She was too busy bobbing up and down. The top of her head being all that Grayson could see at the moment. "I'm going to come," he shouted. "Yes, yes!" He had given her a warning, but she didn't seem to care. She continued sucking, making him crazy the harder she pulled. All of a sudden, it was too late, he couldn't hold back anymore. He came, overflowing in her mouth. She didn't draw back; in fact, she embraced it and swallowed it all. He was amazed and owed her a great deal of gratitude. It had been a long time for him, longer than he would have wanted anyone to know.

Jordan stood up, giving Grayson a knowing glance. He saw that she had met her pleasure as well by the wet stain on her shorts. She smiled. He wasn't quite sure what do say or do next.

She had made all the moves. Should he gesture her to the bedroom? Maybe that was assuming too much. "Grayson, I'm not sure what you're thinking, but everything is fine." He felt a little relieved, but he still wasn't sure what he should say. "I'm sorry, this is just a little awkward. If this was my place, I would ask you if you wanted to stay or continue in the bedroom, but this is your show." She giggled. "That's a little fast for me," she said, giving him a wink. "The bathroom is right through there if you want to clean up a bit. I'll be right back." He nodded and watched her head upstairs before getting up to head for the bathroom. He wasn't sure what had just happened. He knew what happened, but she seemed unphased. Was she just doing him a favor, was he that obvious? He blew out a frustrated sigh as he opened the bathroom door. As good as it was, it felt kind of empty now. He at least thought she would have invited him upstairs. Now he had created a sticky mess, in the literal sense as well. He knew that he would be in trouble if anyone found this out. He would make sure he kept it under wraps; he could only hope that she did the same. Even if he couldn't ask her to. If the wrong people found out that was the end of his career. There would be no questions asked. He wanted to regret it, but he didn't. He wanted to take her upstairs and show her what he could do, obviously, that wasn't her idea. He quickly cleaned himself up and returned to the sofa. Jordan hadn't come down yet.

Jordan looked at her face in the mirror. Her lips were swollen from Grayson's kisses. She had to admit, the Investigator knew what he was doing. He had the makings of one fantastic night, but not yet. This was just the beginning. She loved the way he looked, with his head thrown back and eyes closed. His moans stoked her fire so much she came just from the blow she gave. She didn't mean for that to happen, but she was into it. She wanted Grayson, more than any man in a long time. If he wasn't a cop, things might be different. But he was, and they couldn't be. She had thrown down the gauntlet. She had a piece of leverage that she could use to her advantage. If things got out of hand, she'd just get another piece. It seemed very easy. He was more than willing to give, and she was oh so ready to receive. She hurried into her bathroom and refreshed herself. She was certain she would find him waiting for her, and she had to have her game face on.

Grayson turned as he heard Jordan coming down the stairs. She had changed into what looked to be some pajamas. "I know you're probably confused about what just happened here, but don't be," she said. He just continued to watch her without saying anything. "I would like to see more of you, Grayson, much more," she said, patting his hand as she sat down. "This wasn't a onetime deal. I've been feeling things for you since the first time we met. I just knew that it was wrong for me to act on it. Wrong for me and for you, but tonight I just couldn't resist. I needed you. I hope you understand." He smiled. He was happy that this wasn't just one of those things. He really liked Jordan, but he was no fool. He knew the consequences if this got out. He did, however, appreciate her coming at him with the truth. He was glad it wasn't a game she was playing.

"I do," he said. "I needed you too. I think that is one of the things that drove me here tonight. I would like to see more of you too. I hope to as soon as we can clear up these investigations."

"Do you know how much longer I will be under speculation," she asked, giving him puppy dog eyes. "It's hard to say. We have to check out everyone," he replied. "I hate that you are involved. I know it's hard on you." She looked away quickly. "Hey," he said, putting his hand on her shoulder. "I'll make sure it gets over as fast as it can. I know you just want your life to go back to normal. I'll stay out of your hair, and I'll make sure Victoria does too." "I would be very grateful for that," she replied.

"How well do you know Victoria?" "She and I have been partners for the past three years. She is very good at what she does. She's a friend," Grayson replied. Jordan felt a pang of jealousy.

"She seems to be very thorough," she replied.

"Did she say something that upset you this morning," he asked, looking at her seriously. "I can speak to her about that. She is protective of me, and sometimes she speaks before she thinks, but she is a good cop."

"No, she just asked a lot of questions. She seemed hell-bent on me being involved," she said. "Hmmmm," said Grayson. "She was just upset with me. I think that was her main reason for coming here. She knew I would be angry about it. Don't worry about Vicki. Her bark is far worse than her bite, and she only bites people who absolutely deserve it." Grayson laughed. She didn't.

"Well, I guess I'll be turning in," said Jordan. "Another busy day tomorrow." "Me too," he said, standing. "Thank you for coming by, Grayson," she said, giving him a hug and a kiss on the cheek.

"No problem," he replied, giving her the dimple again. "Hopefully, the next time you see me, it won't be on such terrible circumstances."

"I hope not," she said, standing in the doorway. "Please drive safely."

"Sure will," he said as he crossed the road.

Fourteen

Jordan closed the door smiling. She had succeeded. Poor Grayson, he was a sex-starved idiot. Most men were. He had already vowed to keep her name out of both these investigations and wrap them up as fast as possible. He also said he would keep that nosey ass Victoria Evans out of her hair, all from a blow. Sometimes you outdo yourself, she said, patting her mouth. She pretty much had Grayson Jeffcoat by the balls. He would do her bidding. He didn't have a choice; one allegation of misconduct would have him tossed off the force and end his stellar career. She felt a tad bad saying that. She really hoped that she wouldn't have to ruin Grayson. She did like him. He was different. He seemed to really be looking out for her. He had never made any reference to her wealth in any conversation they had. It almost seemed as though he was ignorant of it. He was so gullible it was almost funny. She would use whatever she needed to. That wasn't a problem for her. If he got hurt, he got hurt. He should be smarter. Lucky for her, he wasn't.

Grayson headed straight home after he left Jordan's. He believed a little in love at first sight. He was one hundred percent certain about lust at first sight. With Jordan, he felt a little of the first one and a lot of the second one, but there was another emotion at play within him. Suspicion. He had gone to her house with a genuine thought, he wanted to make sure she was ok. He wouldn't play a victim and say that she made him do anything. That was a real sweet bonus for him. But Grayson knew she was up to something. He had wanted her too. That wasn't a secret, but she had been very indifferent to him. You don't just go down on people you're indifferent to. He enjoyed it way too much, so did she. He knew it wasn't just for pleasure. It was a means to an end. As soon as he came, she was cold again. Her mind calculating the next move. When she came back downstairs, she did two things that were red flags for him. She wanted to know how much longer he would be investigating her, and she was quick to say she wanted to see him. She also didn't like Vicki poking around. She made sure to let him know that. It was apparent to him that she used sex to get her way a lot. She didn't have to, but some women operate that way. She probably had the idea that that was the best way to control men. It hurt his feelings a little to think he could be controlled that way. Bad thing for her, he wasn't wired that way. Sure, he would love a roll in the sack with her. She was beautiful, sexy and he thought she was a good person, damaged, but good overall. That being said, she couldn't change his opinions or the facts. He had never covered up anything he found during an investigation, and he wouldn't start now. It didn't matter how sweet she tasted, or how much she batted those pretty brown eyes.

The next few days were confusing for Jordan. She hadn't seen or heard from Grayson since he left her house that night. She thought for sure he would have called at least once, wanting to see her again. Maybe she had underestimated him. That was highly doubtful, or so she had thought up until now. What was he doing? Had he found something else? She really couldn't find out. She didn't have any eyes or eyes in the precinct. She steered clear of cops as much as possible. It just didn't set well with her current pastime. She was absolutely sure she would have bedded Grayson Jeffcoat by now. Maybe he figured her out. He seemed to buy the whole thing, and she knew he wasn't acting. He was taken by her, and he wanted more. So where had he disappeared to? She had to find out what he was doing, but she wasn't sure how. She had limited resources as far as people she could count on. He had already met Carly, so she was out of play. She thought to herself, maybe Lamar would be interested in doing some acting.

Grayson had been keeping himself busy. He had really buckled down on the Anderson case. He questioned more of David's neighbors. None of them knew much. He went back to his workplace, he even checked into his bank accounts. He continually came up empty. There were no strings, no stray ends. Whoever killed David Anderson did it for a personal reason. They didn't leave any clues behind. That also let Grayson know that they had killed before. A person who was new at this would have left something. They would have been messy. This was not messy. It was quick and clean. Anderson, the poor bastard, had really got himself mixed up with the wrong dudes. Grayson thought to himself about the list of unsolved murders back at the precinct. He would have to check them out. He would have to see if any of the suspects in those murders could have come across David Anderson. He doubted it. His gut was telling him that wasn't where to look, but it wasn't navigating where. He had to figure it out. Somewhere, a killer was hiding in plain sight, and he had to find them.

Grayson also felt bad about what was happening between him and Victoria. She found out he had been snooping around her crime scene, and she wasn't speaking to him. Women, he thought. It didn't matter that she had done the same thing. She was angry at him. She said he had his head up his ass. Maybe she was right, but he didn't have the time or energy to address it. She should be happy with that. By him digging in on her case, he might find something to help her out. She didn't care about that right now. Grayson Jeffcoat was an asshole, that was her mentality. He was caught up with this rich girl. That was what he had going on. He didn't have time to do real police work. That was far from the truth. All he had been doing as of late was police work. He hadn't had any contact with Jordan Chandler since that fateful night. That night had frustrated him to no avail. It had made him want to call her every night, but he knew he couldn't. He had crossed the line. Plus, it didn't help that he had the feeling that she would use it against him if need be. He had avoided Victoria at every turn. She had got tired of calling him after he ignored enough of her calls. When he got to work, if he saw her car, he didn't bother going in. He would just come back after hours. He would fix it with her somehow, but right now, other things had to be handled.

"What's up, Mike," said Lamar as he answered his cell. "I've got another job for you, but I'm not sure if you are going to be interested," said Jordan. "Sounds interesting already. What is it, and why won't I be interested?"

"I need you to get in with a cop for me. A female cop." Her voice trembled a little. "Why," he asked. "Has she made you, us?"

"No, she's working Lizzie's case, and she seems a little overzealous for my liking. She's been here once, and I don't want her to come back. I just need someone to find out what she knows."

"How do you suppose I do that," Lamar asked. "You know acting isn't my strong suit."

"You don't have to act," said Jordan. "Just charm her. She's young and attractive. I get the feeling she's not seeing anyone. She seems a bit too preoccupied with other people for that to be an issue."

"Preoccupied," he said. "Who is she?"

"Her name is Investigator Victoria Evans. She's Grayson Jeffcoat's partner," she replied. "His partner. I don't like where this is going, Mike. It seems like some bitch shit to me. You must really have it bad for him. Is she fucking him?"

"No, and it's not some bitch shit. Besides, I don't pay you to like Lamar, I pay you to do," she replied. "I'll give you double this time."

"Double," he said. "Yeah, you got it bad. What exactly do you need me to do."

"I need you to find out what she has on us. I need to know everything she has gathered from Lizzie's and if we can be made. That's all. If she doesn't have anything, you can remove yourself from the situation," Jordan replied. "But if she does," he asked. "Then, you have to kill her, simple as that." There was dead silence on the line.

"Kill her. Kill a woman and a cop; you know I can't do that. Not even for double," he said. "Fine," Jordan replied. "If you find out she knows something, just let me know. I'll kill her. It may give me some pleasure."

"You know, Mike, you're one sick girl. Maybe you should seek some counseling," he said. Jordan chuckled. "Been there, done that," she replied. "I don't care how you get in, just do it. If you need any money for expenses, let me know. I don't know where she lives yet, but if she's not at the precinct, she frequents a little coffee shop about two blocks away from there. Maybe you could run into her there. I have no doubts you have what it takes." She could feel his smile through the phone. All men loved their egos stroked. Even hardened criminals.

106

"I'll see what I can do," said Lamar. "I'll let you know something in a few days."

"Ok, but, Lamar, I really need you to get on this. Time is a luxury we don't have, and I do mean we." "I'm on it, Mike and trust me, I know you mean time is a luxury I don't have. No one is going to lock up a pretty little rich girl. And you would throw me under the bus, I've been aware of that from the first deal we made. I'm no idiot." Jordan didn't reply. She knew Lamar was right. She liked him. He worked neat and clean, and he was as trustworthy as they come. She wouldn't want to see him in prison. She would hire the best defense money could buy for him. Because if push came to shove, it would be him. He was the sacrificial lamb, and the sad thing about our society is that they would readily accept him with not many questions asked. If any. "I'll wait to hear from you," she replied before quickly pressing end.

Fifteen

Victoria Evans's life was getting stranger by the day. She had been dying to tell Grayson what she had found out in regards to the handkerchiefs, but he had been avoiding her. He would say he was working, too busy to answer her calls, but she knew he was avoiding her. He was never in the office when she was there anymore. He either came in early or came back late. She knew she had rubbed him the wrong way. She had no business sticking her nose in his private affairs. She couldn't help herself. She saw something bad happening for him, and it wore couture suits. She had to help him, even if he didn't want it. She had basically come to a standstill on her investigation. The handkerchiefs were a great lead, but that was all she had and she didn't know who they belonged to. She heard that Grayson had been out to the estate and talked with someone, but he hadn't been around for her to find out what he knew. She did know, however, that the hankies didn't belong to their suspect. Not that she expected them to. They had his prints, and she didn't believe he knew anything about David Anderson's murder, and that was where she had found the first one.

A few nights ago, she had finally joined Teddy for that drink after work. She had to admit that it had turned out better than she thought, but she couldn't see herself with Teddy. He was very sweet. He even walked her to her door when she told him he didn't have to. He lingered a bit in the doorway as if he had expected her to ask him in. She didn't. It wasn't because he wasn't attractive enough. He was, but she was still holding that place in her heart for someone else, in her bed as well. She looked over at Grayson's desk. It looked like he hadn't been there in days. There were no doodles on the end of his pad, something he did when he was nervous, or Styrofoam cups from his hot chocolate habit. She wanted to make it right with him, but she didn't know how. She was stubborn, and it took a lot out of her to admit her failings. It was a horrible flaw, but she was honest about it. She drew her eyes away from his empty desk. She wished to hear him laugh right now or see his blue-gray eyes staring back at her, even in anger.

He would come around soon. She just had to give him his space. She decided she would go home. Sitting there pining did nothing for her, and it definitely wasn't getting anything done.

"Hi, Grayson, this is Jordan. I was just checking on you this time. I hope I didn't scare you off the last time you were here. I hope your feelings aren't hurt. I would have called before now, but I've just been busy. Anyway, give me a call when you're free." Jordan had left a message for him. It was weird. Not so much what she said, but that she would leave one. She didn't seem like that type, plus for as long as she had his card, this was the first time she had called. She had expected to hear from him before now. She was getting anxious. If her plan had worked, he was due back there in a day or two after their moment. He hadn't come back. He hadn't even called. She wasn't expecting that. This was why she reached out.

He wasn't sure how he should play it. He didn't want to let on, but he didn't want to go back to her house. He knew what the next stage of the plan was. He thought about that for a second. Sweet, sexy Jordan underneath him while he pounded her into the mattress. That was a lovely thought, but also a reckless one. His body paid no attention to his last remark. He would call her back. If she wanted to meet, he would choose a public place. Being alone with her would only hurt his case and his career. Even with what he was feeling right now, he had to admit he never thought she was guilty. He never did. She admitted being in David Anderson's apartment several times. She called 911 when she found him, she didn't have to do that. The only thing that even tied her to Elizabeth Beckett's murder was the fact that she knew her and that she had a strong dislike for the woman. But who could blame her after her lifetime of experiences with her? Grayson admitted to himself that if it was him, he wouldn't like her either. Jordan Chandler was hiding something. He was sure of that, what he wasn't sure of was what it was. He had to find that out without getting into her bed. Could he find out without that, or would he be forced to turn her plan around and use sex to get her to reveal it to him? That made him snicker. Now he was going to resort to sexpionage. He wasn't that desperate. Not just yet. But he was willing to admit he would make that sacrifice for the team if needed.

"Hey, Vicki," said the stocky man behind the counter. "What can I get you?" "The usual, Ralph. It's just been one of those days," she replied. He nodded in agreement. "A cop's life isn't a pretty one," he said. "But you still are. What are you now twenty-four, twenty-five?" Ralph always had a way to make Victoria smile. He knew she had passed her twenties a while back, but he tried that line at least once a week.

"Here you go," he said, returning with a large cup of coffee and a piece of apple pie. "You know you do need to eat real food," Ralph said. "Why don't you come over and let me cook you a good hot meal?" "I don't think Julie would go for it, Ralph," said Vicki. "She would have both our heads." "She wouldn't mind. She would more than likely welcome the company," he said. "Besides, you could bring that boyfriend of yours along. She would thank me a million times. She loves to look at him. She says he looks too good to be getting shot at."

"Grayson's not my boyfriend," Vicki said. "I've told you two that." "I know, I know," Ralph said. "But we're old, and we want young people to be in love. We see how you look at him. You love him." Victoria began cutting her pie. "You can't deny it. Even the pie knows," said Ralph.

"Where's lover boy anyway. I haven't seen him around. You two are like peas in a pod."

"I don't know. I haven't seen him in a couple of days. We had a fight, sort of," said Vicki. "A fight, you two. I can't believe it," he said. "But cheer up, it happens to the best of us. He'll come around. He would be a fool not to."

"He most definitely would be," said the stranger sitting down on the stool next to her.

"Excuse me," he continued, "I'm sorry to butt in, but I couldn't help but overhear you. I don't know what you did, but he would be doing you a grave disservice by not making up with you." Victoria blushed. "It could be the biggest mistake of his life or the greatest reward for me." She blushed again.

"Do I know you," she asked. "You may, or I may just have that type of face," he replied. "Let's do this officially. Hi, I'm Lamar." He extended his hand to shake hers. "And you would be?" "Victoria, Victoria Evans," she replied, shaking his hand. "Good grip. I like that." He turned to his menu and began to look it over. Ralph shook his head and moved down to the end of the counter to speak with a few of his other regular customers.

"Do you do that a lot," Victoria asked, turning on her stool towards Lamar. "Do what," he responded, looking up from his menu. "Make charming comments to take over conversations of people you just met?" He turned on his stool to face her. "No. I save that for beautiful women I want to get to know, and before today, it was just a line I practiced in the mirror. I knew it would come in handy if I ever met a woman worthy of using it on. You're the first." Victoria could feel her face going warm again. She didn't want it to, but it did. "Thank you. I'm glad your hard work has paid off for you." Lamar placed the menu on the counter.

"You're funny too. I like a woman with a sense of humor. The world seems too serious at times." Victoria went back to playing with her pie. "My world is serious all the time," she said. "It comes with the territory." "I've heard that comment before," he said. "I guess you have one of those highly stressful jobs. You can sometimes guess a person's occupation by observing them."

"Really," said Victoria. "Go ahead, give it a try." "Well, originally, I would have guessed model. Your cheekbones are amazing, but I don't think you've starved enough for that. My second guess would have been lawyer, but I don't see a briefcase, I-pad or cell phone in sight. So, I'm going to go with doctor or cop. My god, I hope you're not a cop." Victoria opened her jacket just a bit and showed him her shield on her belt buckle and gun in her shoulder holster.

"Well, I was right," Lamar said. "A woman with a gun and a badge, I imagine some handcuffs are a part of this ensemble as well." She nodded in agreement. "But, I'm torn now." "Why," asked Vicki. "Well, I really hate to think about someone shooting at a woman as beautiful as you, but I'm also thinking about you making all my sexy cop fantasies come to life.

112

What's a man to do?" She smiled again. This had been the most smiling she'd done in a while, and for once, it wasn't Grayson as the source. "You're funny too," she said, flashing Lamar a smile. "Humor works for both genders."

"Can I get you something, sir," said Ralph as he made his way back to them. "What do you recommend," he asked Vicki. "I was so mesmerized by the lovely Victoria I didn't have time to look at the menu," he said to Ralph. "Everything here is good," she replied. "I eat here all the time."

"She does, her and her boyfriend, he's a really big guy around your size," interjected Ralph. Victoria shot him a look. "I'm sorry, Victoria. I didn't know you were taken," said Lamar. "I'm not," she said. "The guy he's speaking of is just my partner. Ralph has a funny sense of humor too. Don't you, Ralph?" Ralph smiled and shrugged his shoulders. "Well, in that case, I'll have what she's having. And you're right, Victoria, everything here is good." There was that damn smile again.

"Are you from around here," Vicki asked finally getting a piece of the pie in her mouth. "I actually just got into town a few days ago," he said. "What do you do," she asked, signaling the waitress to refresh her cup of coffee. "I'm a recruiter for the NFL. I'm here to check out a few university standouts. Football is something I love. It was my life until I got injured, so the boys were nice enough to give me something to keep me busy that allowed me to do what I loved," he said. "So, football still pays the bills." Victoria was listening intently.

"Was being a cop your first choice," he asked.

"It was," she said. I come from a line of cops. My granddad and my dad were cops. Two of my brothers are firemen. My oldest brother, however, is a dentist." Lamar laughed aloud. "A dentist, really?" he said. "Yes," she replied. "He went to college and got as far away from the rest of us as he could. He said danger wasn't for him. My mother, however, hates that I'm a cop. This isn't something she wanted for her only daughter. She would always say, "I hope you don't marry a cop." She didn't count on me becoming one."

"Maybe you should consider marrying an ex-football player," said Lamar taking a sip of his coffee.

Sixteen

The next day Grayson had gotten to the station early. He had calls to make, and truthfully, he was tired of avoiding Victoria. There were things he needed access to that were only at the station, like those handkerchiefs to begin with. He had lucked out. He had been there for an hour, and she hadn't showed yet. He was happy to avoid the headache. He really wasn't in the mood for one of her tirades, especially in front of everyone. She had no filter. That was one of their love/hate things. It was awesome when she went off on someone else, but not so much when he was in the line of fire.

All of a sudden, he heard whistles and catcalls behind him. What was going on now? The captain had warned them about the sounds they made when the prostitutes were brought in. The men still showed their appreciation sometimes. He had no doubt that some of them were regular customers. Andrew motioned his head to the left with a lustful gleam in his eye. He really didn't want to look back. He had things to do, and watching whoever just came in wasn't on the agenda. Before he could turn his head, the topic of discussion came into view. It was Victoria who was causing the entire ruckus.

Grayson wanted to be angry, but the vision that stood next to him dried his mouth like cotton. There stood Vicki in a way he had never seen before. Her black hair was curled into layers that fell past her shoulders. It shimmered like silk. He had never seen her without her ponytail or bun. She never wore her hair down. She considered it a work hazard. She was wearing makeup that accentuated the beauty of her face. He had always considered Victoria to be attractive, but she was gorgeous. She wore a purple dress that molded to her curves and stilettos. Another item he thought she didn't know existed. He couldn't take his eyes off her, and she knew it.

"Hi," she said, sitting down at her desk. "Hi," he replied. "You look beautiful." He wanted to say something, but he wasn't sure if that was it.

But he couldn't help it. That was how she looked.

"Thanks," she replied. "So, do you." He smiled.

"Look, I'm sorry," he said. "I know I haven't been a good friend here of late. I won't give excuses. I just want us to go back to the way we were." "I missed you too, Gray," she said. "We're good." He knew she meant it so he wouldn't follow it up with a long drawn out speech. "So are you undercover or something," he asked. "I'd never make you. I'd be too busy trying to find out who you were." She gave him a weird look.

"No, no undercover work for me," she replied. He gave her a funny look. "Then what's all this about," he asked, moving his hand up and down in reference to her outfit. "I have a date after work. I'm on desk duty, but we are going downtown, so I wouldn't have time to go home and change." Grayson got a funny feeling in his gut. Date is another word that wasn't a part of Victoria Evans's vocabulary. She always said men were more trouble than they were worth. All except him, and he was not the person taking her out. He was feeling a little jealous. What had he missed in the last few weeks?

"A date," he asked. "Do I know him?" "No," she said. "He's not a cop." "I know more than cops," he said, sounding a little defensive.

"Really," she asked. "Name someone that you really know that isn't a cop." He thought for a minute, but he couldn't give an answer. "See, that's what I thought," she continued.

"Where did you meet this guy," Grayson asked. "At Ralph's," Vicki replied. "You're asking a lot of questions for someone who is not interested." "I'm just making sure he's not a bum, you know looking out," he said. "Yeah, I know," Victoria said with a smile. Even though he would never admit it, she could see the jealousy in his face. She was flattered. For all the remarks and invitations she had given Grayson Jeffcoat, he hadn't taken her up on any of them. Now here he was looking at her like this was his first time seeing her and being testy because she was going on a date. What nerve!

"What's his name? What does he do," Grayson asked, continuing with his interrogation. "His name is Lamar, and that is the last of your questions," she said, smiling like the cat that swallowed the canary.

He knew she meant that. "If you like, Gray, we can go out next week if this doesn't work out," she said. Grayson just turned around in his chair. She was trying to bait him. He knew it. There was really no reason he shouldn't date Victoria other than the fact that they were partners. That was usually a no-no. She had asked him a thousand times, and he had blown her off a thousand times. He knew she was serious, but he didn't want to mess up their friendship. Or that was what he kept telling himself. He had no reason to be jealous. She had made her intentions clear a long time ago, and he had been a chicken. He would have to bite this one and watch how it played out. He had no reason to block her happiness, especially when he was hoping that once Jordan was cleared, he could see what could develop there. He was being such a baby right now.

"Jeffcoat, I need you in my office, stat," yelled the Chief from a crack in his door. Grayson jumped up from his desk and hurried over to his office. He hated when the Chief yelled at him, but he couldn't have called him at a better time.

Victoria watched Grayson's back as he went into the Chief's office. She knew that when Grayson didn't respond, she had gotten him. She knew he wasn't going to. He wasn't going to say yes, nor was he going to make up an excuse as to why he couldn't. He was just going to ease the conversation on to something else. He did that a lot. Victoria knew he was lonely. She felt that this was one of the reasons he was so gung ho about Jordan's innocence. He was interested in her. That made her heart fall a little. She still had to tell him about the handkerchiefs, but not today. He might feel she was rubbing something in his face. It could wait. She didn't want to make him upset since they had mended their break, and she didn't want to spoil her evening. If they had another blow-up, she would either cancel her date or spend the whole night worrying about his feelings. She wasn't going to do it, not tonight. She deserved this date, and she was going to enjoy it.

"You're going on a date with her tonight," Jordan asked Lamar. "Yeah, I'm going to take her to Chez Nouveau. We have reservations at eight," he replied.

"Chez Nouveau, that's kind of expensive," she said. "Can you cover that?"

"Yeah, Mike," he said, sounding irritated. "You pay me enough to afford it. I hope she doesn't have anything on you." "Why," she replied, sounding equally irritated. "Because she's a cool girl," he said. "You didn't say she was beautiful. I'd hate for you to have to kill her." Jordan didn't say anything. "You just make sure you find out what she knows, Lamar," she said. "It's for both our sakes." Lamar didn't say anything. He just hung up. Jordan didn't like that. She didn't take Lamar for one of these love-struck types. He never said anything about it, but then again, she never asked him about his personal life. This made her feel a little uneasy about Lamar. He had never seemed hesitant to do anything, not for her. She sat for a moment and composed herself. She had to go on a little recon mission before Lamar's date. She had to make sure everything went according to plan.

Grayson's phone rang. It was Jordan. He had to answer this time. He had been avoiding her as well. He didn't call her back the last time she called. "Hello," he said into the phone. "Hi," Jordan purred on the other end of the line. "I thought you had forgotten all about me." He chuckled. "I could never forget about you, Jordan. I'm sorry I haven't had time to come around. There's just been so much work." "I understand," she said, sounding concerned. "How are things going?" "Very slowly," he replied.

"Your fiancé's case will be closing soon due to lack of evidence. I really wanted to find his killer. He didn't deserve to die like that and no one go unpunished. I know you wanted that too." Jordan had to suppress her grin. "I did," she said after regaining control.

"It isn't fair. David never harmed anyone. He was a good person." "I don't know about that," Grayson said. "He did harm you. It still doesn't justify being murdered. I hate unsolved cases." Jordan chose her next words carefully. "I wish things were going better for you," she said. "If there is anything I can do, please tell me."

"There's nothing right now," he said. "Once these things are wrapped up, and I can get some free time, I hope I get a chance to see you again." "Most definitely," she said with glee in her voice. "You just let me know when you're ready. We can make a night of it." Grayson could hear the satisfaction in her voice. "I'll be sure to let you know." "Great," she replied. "Talk to you soon." With that, she hung up the phone. She had found out what she needed to know, or so she thought. He fed her that line of bullshit, and she had bought it. He knew she would. She was almost giddy when he told her that David's case was wrapping up. He didn't like that. Something wasn't adding up. He still didn't want Vicki to be right, but he was certain that she was involved somehow in this case. She hadn't even asked him about Elizabeth Beckett's case this time. That was a plus, but it wasn't much.

Jordan felt as light as air. Grayson Jeffcoat had believed her innocence. He was wrapping up the case with hopes of seeing her when it was done. She wouldn't deny herself or him that pleasure. He deserved it. He had made her problems go away. At least one of them anyway. He hadn't pushed much harder to find out who killed David, not that he would have found anything. She was happy that he believed her. He was easier to control than she thought. She was very proud of herself. She couldn't allow her head to get too big. She had two more stops to make before Lamar went on his date tonight.

Victoria looked up from her desk. She was interrupted by someone clearing their throat. "Excuse me, is Grayson here," she said. She stared back at Jordan with a look of shock and repulsion. "No, he isn't," Victoria replied. "He had some leads to check on." Jordan gave her best sad expression. "That's too bad," said Jordan. "I had really hoped to see him. I had some information he would probably be interested in." Victoria was interested, but she wasn't sure. Jordan could just be lying. She looked like a liar. She did come all the way down there without caring who saw her. "I'm sorry he isn't here," Vicki said. "Can I get you something? Would you like to leave a message for him?"

Jordan gave her a once over. "You look very lovely this evening, Victoria. It is Victoria, isn't it?" Victoria didn't like the idea of her calling her by her first name, but she didn't want her to leave without finding out what she wanted. She had an idea regarding what Teddy said. "It is, and thank you for your compliment," said Vicki. "That shade is pretty on you. You should wear it more often," Jordan replied, giving her a faux smile. "Your message for Gray," Victoria started, "would you like to use my pen?" "Sure," Jordan replied, grabbing the pen from Victoria's hand. "Gray is just the cutest pet name. I told him I was thinking about calling him that myself, but he told me you had already coined the phrase. It suits him perfectly, but that's just like Grayson. Everything about him is perfect. That comment didn't sit well with Victoria. She watched Jordan bitterly as she scribbled a note for Grayson and left it on his desk. "Thank you," Jordan said as she handed the pen back to Victoria. "Please tell Gray I stopped by. I hope that he makes time to see me again." See her again, Vicki thought. So, Grayson's been seeing her? Is that why he stopped talking to her? She couldn't wait to get her hands on him. He had a lot of explaining to do. He knew this was so out of line. "We had so much fun the last time," Jordan continued. She saw her needling was working. She could tell by the expression on the other woman's face. "I'll make certain to let him know you were here," Victoria said flatly. "I'm sure he will be sorry he missed you." Jordan gave her a big smile. "Thank you again, Victoria. If you don't mind, let's just keep my visit between Gray and us. I wouldn't want him to get into any trouble. You know."

"Yeah, I do know," said Victoria. "I'll keep it between us. I don't want him to get into any trouble, either." "Great," Jordan said as she waved goodbye and sauntered out the door, her purse swinging behind her. Victoria didn't like her before, she really didn't like her now. Grayson had been seeing her when he knew the amount of trouble it could cause for him. He was a dummy. She shook her head. She had the nerve to call him Gray. Really, he's my Gray, mine, mine, mine. Victoria was acting like a spoiled brat, and someone had just taken away her favorite doll. Grayson was not a toy, he was a grown man, and she needed to get a grip. Here she was going on a date in a few minutes, and she was fighting mad with a woman over another man that didn't belong to her. No matter how bad she wanted him to, it wasn't the case. She looked down at the pen Jordan left. She took an evidence bag out of the desk drawer and placed it in it, making sure not to touch it where she was holding it. She grabbed her phone. "Teddy, I have something for you. I'll be right down," she said in the receiver. She grabbed the bag and headed downstairs to the lab.

Teddy stared at Victoria through the glass doors. She was so beautiful. He had never seen her in a dress before, and now he knew he would never be able to forget it. "Hey, Teddy," she said, entering the lab. "Hey yourself," he responded. "Don't you look like a million bucks? This must be a real important case you're on." Victoria wasn't sure how to respond. She needed Teddy's help, but she didn't want to lie to him. "It's not for a case, Teddy," she said, deciding to go with the truth. "I'm going on a date." "A date," he said. "I see. So Jeffcoat went ahead and finally made a move. Good for him. I'm not mad. I'm sure you knocked his socks off." Victoria smiled, but she had to correct him. "It's not with Grayson," she said. "It's with someone new. Teddy felt his stomach twist. His feelings were hurt. When he and Victoria had gone for that drink, she wouldn't even invite him into her house, but she was going out with a complete stranger. He didn't like that. He didn't like it at all. "Good for you, Victoria," he said, trying not to show the hurt in his voice. "I hope you have fun. What do you have for me?"

"This," she said, showing him the pen in the evidence bag. "Do you remember when I was here last week, and you told me if I could get the print of the person that I thought the handkerchiefs belonged to you could match it?" Teddy nodded in remembrance. "This is it. I just got it a minute ago. My prints should be the only other ones you find, but I only handled it from the very top." Teddy took the evidence bag from her and placed it on his desk. Victoria could see he wasn't happy with her going on her date. "Teddy, I'm sorry," she said. "It's not you. It's me, and I know that's so cliché, but it really is me. Please don't be angry at me." Teddy didn't say anything. He just kept his back to her. She hadn't wanted to hurt Teddy, but she owed him the truth even if he wasn't going to be happy with it.

Victoria didn't say anything more. She just left the lab.

Grayson returned to the precinct to find it pretty much empty. He looked over on his desk and found an envelope with a sticky note attached to the front of it. "This is from your girlfriend. She came by," the note read. It was from Victoria. She had said girlfriend, so he assumed it was from Jordan. He could feel Victoria's anger in her writing. She'd be pissed again when he saw her. He really was hoping otherwise, but he knew better. He opened the envelope. It was a note written on a piece of department stationery. "I came by to see you, but you were out. I took a chance on you just like you did on me. I hope to see you again soon. Love, Jordan. P. S. I don't think she likes me." There was an arrow drawn pointing in the direction of Victoria's desk. Jordan came by here. She risked the paparazzi and paid me a visit. That was weird. Either she was genuine in wanting to see him, or she was trying to find something out. To catch him off guard. Victoria had been there. He wondered how much she had told her. He would love to believe she didn't tell her anything, but he knew that Jordan was the kind who would rub something in someone's face even if she had to do it in small increments. He would have preferred she knew nothing. She was going to pitch a fit just by knowing that he had any type of involvement with her. He could tell she was angry by the strength in her writing. She would have a right to. It was unethical and just stupid, but he had done it, and what's done is done.

Seventeen

Chez Nouveau was an elegant restaurant. It was candlelit and the ambiance was perfect for a first, romantic date. "You look wonderful," Lamar said as he pulled the chair out for Victoria. "Thank you, so do you," she said. Lamar was quite handsome in his black suit. He had made an extreme effort to pull out all the stops.

"I was so glad you agreed to come out with me this evening, Ms. Evans," he said. "I thought I had come on too strong for you." Victoria laughed. "You were strong, but not too strong," she replied. "I like a man who isn't afraid to go after what he wants. Some men aren't that strong." She felt that her last comment was a dig at Grayson.

"This is a nice place. It's my first time coming here," she said. "Mine too," replied Lamar. "It was listed in my welcome to the city brochure. It had five stars, so I thought, why not?" "I think it was worth every one so far," said Victoria taking a sip of her red wine. "Why are you looking at me like that?" "You have taken my breath away, Victoria," Lamar said, touching her hand across the table. She liked the way that felt. She hadn't been on a date in a long time and planned to enjoy everything that went with it. "So, tell me what interesting cases are you working on? We can talk about what I do later. It's in no way as exciting as what you do," said Lamar. Victoria laughed. "Only some of it is exciting," she said. "The rest of it is just paperwork. That's one of the things I hate about investigations." "I can agree. Paperwork sucks for everyone. For all this paperless stuff they talk about, I find myself doing more and more paperwork," he said. "I heard on television that you are the lead investigator on the murder of that millionairess, Elizabeth Beckett. How's that going for you?"

"It's had some up and down moments," she said. "We have a suspect. He was caught red-handed, but a lot of people believe he is innocent. We had him in custody, but he made bail. We are still searching; besides, he didn't have a motive." "So is he your only lead," Lamar asked. "For now, he is," she replied. "We don't have any more suspects, just weird occurrences." "What type of occurrences," asked Lamar. "Well, we have found a piece of evidence that ties the murder I'm working on with one my partner is working on as well." "That is interesting," said Lamar. "What type of evidence is it, if I can ask that," asked Lamar. "I can't say what it is," said Victoria, "but I can say that we found one at both of the crime scenes. All I have to do now is find the missing piece that puts it together. I'm almost there." She smiled. It made her happy to know that Lamar was interested in her job. Her exes had seemed to be resentful of her being a cop. They didn't like that she wouldn't be available for their needs. "That's great, Vicki," he said. "I hope you find your "missing link." They continued to have a great conversation until their food came.

Jordan made herself comfortable from the rooftop of a building across the street from Chez Nouveau. She had gotten a great roof view so that she could see whenever they left the restaurant. She had a surprise for Victoria Evans. She didn't like her. She was annoyed by her presence. She didn't like the way she seemed to think it was ok to nose about in everyone's business. She also didn't like the ownership she saw in her eyes when it came to Grayson Jeffcoat. She read much more than friend when they had spoken earlier that day. What Victoria didn't know was that Jordan had heard her entire conversation. Lamar had allowed her to bug him just in case she gave away any interesting information. She wanted to know firsthand if she had something on her. That way, if need be, she could get rid of it while they were out. She did reveal that they had something. She just didn't say what it was. Jordan continued to listen.

"So, you have something," Lamar said. "Will it be enough to bring the person you suspect in?" "If everything adds up, it will be," said Victoria making a worried expression. "Why that look, Sweetie," he asked. "It's nothing," she replied. "Sure, it is. That's the first time I've seen you frown since I've known you," he said. Victoria gave him a shy smile.

"It's just that if what I have is the key to my investigation, it's going to be big. Really big." "Oh, I see," he responded. "Some bigwig is the suspect." "I didn't say who it was," she implored. "It's just that some innocent people will get hurt, and for others, it would change their lives considerably."

"Well," Lamar started, "you can't just go around killing people and not expect it to have some type of negative impact on your life."

"People do it every day," Victoria said. "They just don't think about getting caught. It's amazing what a few handkerchiefs can prove." "Handkerchiefs," Lamar asked. "Disregard that last comment. It's just a theory. Let's talk about you," she said, taking a bite of her steak. Lamar smiled and began a story about his life.

"Handkerchiefs," Jordan said atop the rooftop, her mind reeling to figure out what she meant. If she found a handkerchief of hers at David's, so what. She was in and out of there, but what about Lizzie's. Where did she get a handkerchief there? She thought to herself. She didn't remember ever having one there. "Fuck," she said aloud. She had one in her back pocket. It had probably fallen out in the closet. She hadn't thought to look for it when she got home. She had just thrown her clothes in the closet, and she didn't tell Lamar to sweep the closet. They had her. The handkerchief from the closet not only had her fingerprints but some of her DNA. She needed to get them back. She knew where they were. She saw one on Grayson's desk in a plastic bag. She assumed that it was the one that had to do with her case. That was the one from David's apartment. She didn't see the other one, the one from Lizzie's. Victoria had to have it. It had to be near or around her desk. She would use it to ruin her. She knew it. Lamar had done good. He had served her well. Too bad, he was going to be a casualty. He was a trusted friend, but she couldn't have loose ends. She just couldn't. He knew the risks. He knew her temper, but it had never been aimed at him. She hated to do it, but she was caught. If she didn't do it, he would spend the rest of his life in prison. He would have to. Even if she would too, she would have to give him up. She would need to make a deal. She was rich and had a company to run. She could deal with a little blemish, a slap on the wrist. But what she couldn't do was leave her legacy to a bunch of imbeciles who would more than likely divide it and sell pieces of it to the highest bidder. Not in her life would that happen.

She heard laughter. Lamar and Victoria were leaving the restaurant. They seemed happy. Lamar told her that he liked Victoria. She had felt good about that. No one should have to spend their whole life in this game. Lamar was good at what he did, but she didn't want this to be his life. Too bad it had been. She had chosen this path for herself a long time ago. She didn't mean to bring anyone down with her, but there were just some things she couldn't do for herself. Lamar opened the passenger side door for her. They had taken his car. He had given her a kiss before closing the door. That was sweet. Victoria would remember that for the rest of her life. Lamar quickly drove away. Jordan pushed the button on the detonator in her hand. They were no more than one hundred feet away from her when she blew Lamar's car to bits. She watched it as the flames danced in a distance. Her eyes welled up with tears. Lamar was her friend, but business was business. He knew if things got bad, sacrifices had to be made. He had just said it himself, "no one could go around killing people and not expect it to have a negative impact on their life." That statement included him whether he knew it or not. He would understand. She felt a sigh of relief that she wouldn't have to deal with Victoria Evans ever again. She apparently was as good a detective as Grayson thought.

She quickly stuffed the detonator in her bag and left the rooftop. Victoria didn't say that she had reported any of this information to Grayson. She had hoped she hadn't, and he could stay in the dark a little longer. She had to get to the station and destroy those handkerchiefs. If they ever did any forensics on them, she would be done for. Grayson was no fool. If he had corroborating evidence, he would do his job. If he ever found out that she was responsible for Victoria's untimely death, he would never forgive her. No amount of fucking would be able to change that. As she walked back to her car, she tried to figure out how she was going to get in. She could just walk in, but she had done that earlier. She didn't need to find Grayson   there. That would breed too much suspicion. She had to get her hands on them.

Grayson had responded to a 911 call from dispatch. So had many others, from what he could see. There were various cops on the scene, along with the fire truck and emergency personnel. "What happened here," he

126

asked a cop at the scene. "Not sure," he said. "From what the civilian who reported it said the car was just driving along and blew up." "What about the driver, how many people were in the car," Grayson asked. "Two," he responded. "No survivors." Grayson walked closer to the smoking car. There was hardly any of it left. He immediately felt sorry for the two passengers. Explosion was one horrible way to die. He hoped they had died on impact. He saw the coroner's van. Ron Green, the county coroner, had just finished zipping up the second bag when he saw Grayson approaching. Ron walked over to the nearest officer and said something, and they both started walking towards Grayson. "Hey Ron, was there anything special about the victims? I saw their car, or rather what was left of it. It wasn't an expensive model. I was hoping there was nothing funny about this. You know how crime families get. I'm kind of up to my ears in murder. I would love for this to just be a random mechanical failure. Not that it discounts the lives lost." Ron gave Grayson a thoughtful look and looked over to the cop at his left.

"Do you mind if I take a look," Grayson asked Ron, pointing to the body bags. "I want to see if I recognize either of them." Grayson started walking, and Ron put his hand up to stop him. "Grayson, you don't want to see what's in those bags," he said. "They're really messed up. The guy nearly got decapitated. You won't be able to recognize him."

"Guy, so they were a couple. Damn. I hope they didn't have any kids," he said. "I'm sure they didn't," said Ron before he knew it. "How would you know that," Grayson asked. "Who is in that bag?" Ron walked over and put his hand on Grayson's shoulder. "We need to talk, Jeffcoat. I need to tell you something." Grayson looked confused.

"Tell me what? Why are you stalling? Who is in that bag, if you don't tell me in two seconds I'm going to walk over there and find out myself." The other officer moved behind Grayson. He wasn't sure what was going to happen since he was not aware of his relationship to the deceased. Grayson looked confused. "That's it, Ron," stepping around him, moving quickly to the bags. When he opened the first one, he outwardly cringed. The man's face was horribly burned on the side he had. The other side had been completely blown off. From what he could tell of him, he didn't recognize him. As soon as he reached the second gurney, he heard Ron behind him. "Grayson, I'm sorry. There was nothing anyone could do." "Sorry about what," he asked, pausing at the zipper. Ron dropped his eyes to the ground.

"It's Evans, Grayson. Victoria's in that bag." Grayson was one hundred percent positive he heard wrong. There was no way in hell that was possible. "What did you say Ron," he asked his voice rising.

"It sounded like you said Victoria is in this bag. That can't be true. She is out on a date having a blast right now."

Ron didn't look up. "I'm sorry, man," he said, motioning for the other cop to move back to where he was standing. Grayson felt tears stinging his eyes. "You're wrong," Grayson shouted. "She is somewhere laughing her ass off right now." There was no reply. The part of his brain that was working knew that Ron wasn't mistaken. He knew Vicki as good as anyone else in the precinct, probably as good as he did since they all graduated from the academy at the same time, but he had to be wrong. How could this have happened? Grayson's hand paused on the zipper. He needed to see her, but it was as if he couldn't will his hands to work.

"Grayson, man, just leave it. Let me take her from this place. Vicki was our friend. She wouldn't want you to see her like that. Let me take care of her." "Is," Grayson replied. "Vicki is our friend." Ron saw the tears rolling down his friend's face. Grayson had lost it. At that moment, before he said another word, Grayson unzipped the bag. There was Victoria. Her hair was matted with blood. Her left cheek was burned. Her dress was burned, and he could see her flesh peeking through the top. Not Victoria, not HIS Victoria. "NO! NO! PLEASE DON'T GO VICKI, PLEASE DON'T LEAVE ME!" Grayson placed his head on Victoria's chest like he was expecting to hear a heartbeat. There was none. Grayson's frame crumbled to the ground, and he began to sob like a newborn child. He had lost the best friend he had ever known.

Jordan watched her television with her morning coffee. It was everywhere on the local stations about Victoria's traumatic death. They were plastering her picture everywhere. Mostly those of her and Grayson. She didn't feel any sympathy. Not for her anyway. She did mourn the loss of her friend Lamar over a bottle of Jack Daniels. She gave his brother the money to pay for a nice funeral. She had even given him a sympathy fuck to make him feel better. She owed Lamar one, so she felt like she was clearing her debt. Grayson was her focal point now. She had never made it back to the station to confiscate the evidence. Now wasn't the right time. She hadn't called. She cared for Grayson, but even in that, she had to handle everything the right way. It was all about timing. Victoria's funeral was going to be held today at five. She wouldn't call today. The timing wasn't right. He loved Victoria. She saw it in his eyes when he talked about her. She didn't think it was a romantic type of love, but the camaraderie they shared was real. He needed time to mourn her properly. If he was too emotional, anything could go wrong. If anything, he wouldn't have time to concentrate on either of the cases. She was sure that he would be taking over Lizzie's since Victoria was done. In her world, it was just another loss of a bitch, nothing to get your feathers ruffled for. She would give Grayson around a week, and then she would check on him. If she was nothing, she was tactful. She had even sent a beautiful arrangement sent to the funeral home that read "With Sympathy." She felt like patting herself on the back. She had gotten away with the murders of four people in less than six months. Well, she wasn't clearly out of the woods on two of them yet. She knew that there was no way to tie her to Victoria and Lamar's murder. They were like bonuses. She couldn't help but feel proud of her accomplishments. Even James would have to tip his hat to her.

Eighteen

Grayson stood looking out the church window. He really didn't want to be there. As a matter of fact, he wished he was anywhere else but there. He still couldn't believe that Victoria was gone. There were so many things he wanted to tell her, none of it became relevant until he wasn't able to. He hated himself for not having that last coffee with her. He let his pride get in the way. He never thought that something like this would happen. They had time. He shook his head. Obviously, that wasn't true since she was gone now. He had made sure that everything for her had been handled as quickly and as dignified as possible. He was the one who called her parents, not the chief. He met them when they came down to the morgue. He had to turn away when her father began to cry. It does something to a man to see another man cry. It had hurt him deeply. Victoria's father had blamed himself for allowing his daughter to become a cop like the rest of her family. Grayson assured him there was enough blame to go around. He just didn't understand it. He could have dealt with it better if it had been in the line of duty. They were cops. No one liked to think about death, but in their line of work, they knew it was highly possible that any day could be that day. No one expected what happened to her. He always told her to be careful whenever she left out without him. He didn't that night. He actually left before her. The chief had sent him on a random errand. He looked down at the white gloves he was wearing. It felt as though they were getting tighter and tighter. He hated them. He hated his dress uniform. He never had to wear it. He was so used to wearing street clothes that this felt unfamiliar. Dress blues meant a fellow officer was lost. This time it was someone close to him, and for the first time in his years on the force, he felt it deeply.

Victoria's family had asked that he say a few words at the service. He didn't want to. Not because he didn't love her but because he did. He felt that his emotions would overtake him once he stood in front of the crowd. He had asked her family if he could stand along with her brother, who was

131

also a cop with the men who would be honoring her with the salute. They agreed. He had hoped that the sounds of gunfire would help to drown out the voice in his head. It was her voice. Victoria had a way with people. She definitely had a way with him. She could compliment him in one breath and curse him out in the next. She was always herself. There was no pretend in her; that was why some people couldn't understand her. She was who she was always. Her family had decided to cremate her. Her body had been so badly burned that her mother refused to bury it. She said it didn't matter if the casket was closed. She didn't want to think about her in the ground that way. They had a beautiful floral urn in the front of the church containing her remains next to a headshot of her in uniform. Her smile beamed out to everyone there. "Investigator Jeffcoat, we are about to begin," said the minister's wife as she stepped out into the vestibule. Grayson nodded in acknowledgment. He felt his palms begin to sweat as he took a step forward. He was going to say goodbye to someone he thought he would never have to say it to, at least not in a forever sense. He sent a silent message to Victoria, letting her know that he would make sure to solve her case. He would make damn sure the killer got what he deserved. He stepped forward, and as soon as he took his seat, the organist began the funeral dirge.

Jordan had bided her time. Or so she thought. It had been two weeks since Victoria's funeral, and she hadn't seen or heard from Grayson. He wasn't answering her phone calls. She had driven out to his home twice, and his truck was there, but she hadn't stopped. She knew he was mourning, but she needed to know what was happening. He was her only way of finding that out now. Grayson had pretty much become a hermit. He had not been to work in a few days. She would give him a little more time, but then she would be seeking answers.

Grayson really couldn't find his place. It had been hard for him to get anything done at work since the funeral. The chief had given him some time off. In that time, he just went over and over the murder scenes and notes from his case and Victoria's. There had to be something he was missing. He had never taken so long to solve anything. He thought he was so sure about some things, but now he wasn't sure about anything. He raked his hand through his hair as he looked at the pictures and reports he had spread out on his dining room table. There had to be a common denominator—one other than Jordan Chandler. Jordan had called him several times since Vicki died. He hadn't answered any of her calls. He didn't have anything to say. He didn't want to listen to what she had to say, even though he had no idea what it was. Who knows, maybe she had news that could break the case. He didn't think that was so, but she had surely called a lot. He ran his hand over his beard, something else that was new to him. He hadn't even shaved. A better cop would have had this solved by now. A better cop would have pulled himself together by now. Too bad that wasn't him. He needed to find something. Anything. These cases were drawing out and neither of them was promising. He needed results. Someone knew something. His phone was ringing. It was Jordan again. This time he decided to answer. "Hello," he said. "Grayson, I'm so glad you answered. I've been worried sick about you," said Jordan. "Sorry," he said. "I didn't mean to worry you. It's just that I've not been talking to anyone. I've just been trying to wrap my head around some things." "I know how you feel," she said. "Experiencing loss is a terrible thing. I know how devastating it can be better than anyone. It's harder when it's someone you loved. I was so sorry to hear about Investigator Evans. I knew you were very close with her." "Thank you," he said. "The flowers you sent were lovely. I really appreciated it. I knew that you weren't that fond of her." "It wasn't that, Gray. She just rubbed me wrong, but I know she was doing her job."

"Jordan," he started, "please don't call me that anymore." "Call you what," she asked cautiously. "Gray," he said shortly. "Victoria started that nickname, and every time I hear it, it just makes me think of her. I don't want to be called that anymore." "I see," said Jordan. "I won't do it again." Grayson thought about the way he had just handled that exchange and felt that an apology was in order. "Jordan, I'm sorry. I don't mean to be short with you. I just have a lot on my mind," he said.

"I understand. I was that way, too," she replied. "Would you like some company?" "No, but thanks for asking," Grayson replied. "Jordan, I have some work to do. Can we talk later?" "Sure," she replied. "Just let me know, and Grayson, you're not alone. I know how you feel." "Thank you," he said. "We will talk again soon." He hung up the phone and sat back in the chair at the dining room table.

Nineteen

Before he could even start again, his phone began to ring. Boy, she doesn't take rejection well, he thought to himself. When he pulled his phone out of his pocket, it was Teddy calling. "Hey, Teddy, what's up," Grayson asked. "Hey, Grayson. I know you've taken some time off to get your mind right, but I have some information for you that you may find interesting," Teddy said. "Can it wait, Teddy? I just don't feel like coming in today," said Grayson. "You need to see this," Teddy replied. "It's something Vicki was working on that involved both of your cases." "I'll be there in twenty minutes," he said, hanging up before Teddy could say anything else.

It took Grayson all of fifteen minutes to make it to the crime lab. He could see Teddy waiting for him through the glass doors. "My god man, you look like shit," he said to Grayson. "It's been hard," he replied. "I know," said Teddy. "I miss her too." Grayson had forgotten about Teddy's crush on Victoria. He instantly felt for the man. He was probably missing her just as much as he was. Maybe even more, but he was still there doing his job. Grayson felt a phantom punch to his gut.

"A few weeks ago, Victoria had a hunch about your cases. She felt that there was a missing link, and she brought me her concerns," Teddy started. Grayson gave him a look. "Don't look at me like that. I guess she never got around to tell you. I told her that I wasn't going to be her fall guy if you found out. She didn't involve you because she knew you wouldn't go along with it." He looked down at the results and smiled. "Well, hell, Victoria. I ended up being your fall guy anyway" He returned his eyes to Grayson.

"She brought me the handkerchiefs and had me run the prints found on them. I found a matching print on both of them, but when I ran it through the system, there wasn't a match, Teddy said. "I asked her if she had any idea who the print belonged to, and she said yes," Teddy continued. "I told her if she could get a print from the person whom she suspected I could run it against the prints I had already and see if they were a match. A few days after that, she brought me this pen." Grayson felt a tug in his heart. "The prints on the pen matched the one found on both the handkerchiefs," Teddy said. "But that's not all. There was some mucus on one of the handkerchiefs, and I took it just in case we needed a DNA match. I used it against the hair samples you brought me. It matched the curly one." Grayson felt his knees buckle. "Grayson, are you alright," Teddy asked.

"Do you know who she had in mind?"

"I do," Grayson replied.

"Well, I'm not certain if this person is your killer, but we have enough evidence to bring them in for questioning. All you have to do is go and pick them up." Grayson's heart dropped into the bottom of his shoes. Victoria had been right all along. She was right, and he didn't listen to her. He knew that was a pen from her desk, the one she had given Jordan to write the note she left for him.

"What are you going to do, Grayson," Teddy asked. "I'll bring her in," he replied. "Teddy, can you get a copy of that report for me. I need it to get a warrant." "Sure, I can have you an official one typed up in about twenty minutes if you can stick around." "Yeah," said Grayson. "I'll be upstairs at my desk." Teddy turned around and started typing feverishly on his laptop. Grayson went out of the lab to the elevators. What was Jordan doing at Elizabeth Beckett's home, in her closet, nonetheless? Was she a killer? She couldn't be. She had no motive, and killers needed motives. They didn't, however, if they were sociopaths. You need some sleep, Jeffcoat, now you're just being crazy. There had to be more to it. When he got to his desk, there was a yellow envelope on it with his name. He looked inside to find a disk that said Beckett House Footage. He guessed Victoria's guys had found that hidden surveillance. He really had to look at it. Hopefully, there would be something on it that would tie everything together.

"Jeffcoat," he heard Andrew say from the corner. "There's a woman out here screaming that she has some information on a murder, but she only wants to speak to you. As Grayson walked over, Stephan leaned in close to him. "You look like hell, man," he said. Grayson just gave him a sideways glance and continued beyond him to see the woman. He was shocked to find Carly, one of Mrs. Beckett's maids. He didn't expect to see her again unless he had to subpoena her to court.

"Carly, I'm here. What's wrong," he asked. "What type of information do you have for me?"

"Investigator Jeffcoat," she said. "I have something to tell you, and I have to tell you now before it's too late. I don't want to end up like Lamar."

"Slow down, Carly," Grayson said. "Who is Lamar, and what does he have to do with my investigation?"

"Lamar's dead and she killed him," Carly said. "I know she did it." Grayson motioned her to the empty seat on the other side of his desk. "Catch your breath, Carly," he said. "I don't have a victim by the name of Lamar. I don't know anyone by that name. Who is he?" "Lamar is my ex, and he was the dude in the car with your partner. She killed them both." Grayson sat back in his seat. "She, she who," he asked. "That rich bitch," Carly screamed. The whole squad room got quiet.

"Ok, start from the beginning," Grayson said. "What does my partner's death have to do with anything?" "Ok, remember when we first met," Carly asked Grayson. "Yeah, it was over at the Beckett estate when I came by with a few questions for the staff, he said. "Right," she continued. "I already knew you were coming. You or that broad that worked with you." Grayson looked at her to see what she was getting at.

"Lamar told me. He said if you all came by, I was to make sure I talked to you. He told me to tell you that I heard Delgado confess. He even paid me ten thousand dollars to do it."

"Why would he do that," Grayson asked. "How did your ex-husband know Delgado?" "He didn't know him, but he knew that he didn't kill that rich old hag. He was there."

"There where? At the estate?"

"Yes," she continued. "He was in the closet. He was the one who made the 911 call." Grayson looked confused. "Did you come here to tell us that your ex-husband killed Elizabeth Beckett?"

"No," she said. "He only came in afterward. She was already dead." "Why was he there if he didn't kill her? You said he was hiding in the closet," Grayson said. "He is a cleaner," Carly said. "He comes in after she kills them. She calls and he comes through and sweeps the place. You know, he gets rid of evidence."

"Are you're saying your ex disposes of evidence for his employer, who is a killer?" asked Grayson. "That's right," said Carly. "She pays him a lot of money. He was really good at what he did." "Did he ever tell you who his employer was," he asked.

"No," she replied. "She was listed in his phone as Mike. I know this because I thought it was his cousin's number and I called it. A woman answered. I went off on him, and he said it wasn't like that. He said it was a code name. He said her first name was the last name of a famous Mike, so that's what he called her." Grayson didn't like what he was hearing.

"You said my partner was somehow involved in this. How?" "The rich woman paid Lamar to hook up with her," she continued. "She needed to find out what you guys had on her. Lamar said she thought that she had someone she could use on the inside, but the deal fell through. So, she needed an alternative plan."

"If Lamar was her cleaner, why would she kill him," Grayson asked.

"I don't know," said Carly. "That's why I'm here. Lamar wanted out. He told me that he was going to go straight. He found himself taking a liking to your partner, and he knew it wouldn't work with her being a cop and all. He said he was going to stop. He had been doing jobs for this bitch on and off since he had to leave the NFL. He had been loyal to her. She didn't like your partner, but she didn't have to kill Lamar too." Grayson looked at Carly's face. He wanted her to be lying, but he knew she wasn't. Her eyes were red and puffy like she had been crying for days. She could have kept this information, but she had come forward with it. He knew what she said was true. He also knew that the rich bitch she spoke of was Jordan Chandler. Victoria had been killed because he was stupid. He should have seen this, but he couldn't. He was blinded by beauty and charm. The hope that a troubled person was just that. Jordan Chandler had played him. She was a sociopath, and at least three people may have lost their lives behind it.

"Why did you decide to come forward now, Carly," Grayson asked. "Lives could have been saved if you had brought this information to me sooner." "Lamar had me swear that I wouldn't tell anyone. She was going to pay him double this time if he got the information she needed. It was going to be enough for both of us to get out. I know that Lamar got her the information. He had allowed her to listen in on their dinner conversation. There was a transmitter in the lining of his jacket. I think that she felt he was going to give her up to your lady friend. That's why she killed him. She couldn't afford any loose ends." Grayson stood up and motioned for a female officer to come over. "Please take Carly to the interrogation room and get a formal statement from her." The officer motioned Carly to a room on the right.

"Investigator Jeffcoat," Carly said before she entered the room. "I'm really sorry about your friend. I didn't know she was going to kill her. When I saw you on the news, my heart went out to ya. It was in your eyes. The hurt was in your eyes. She needs to fry for this." The officer led her into the interrogation room. Grayson punched the desk so hard he felt his knuckle crack. Victoria was dead because of Jordan. She had to pay for that. She was hiding in plain sight all the time. She pretended that she cared about him. He was stupid, and Vicki had paid the price.

He grabbed his jacket. He couldn't wait for the warrant. He had to see her now. "Jeffcoat, where are you going," he heard Stephen ask. He didn't bother answering.

Jordan had just finished writing Grayson's letter. She knew he was aware of what she had done. She saw Carly going into the police station. She was headed there herself to see Grayson, but she stopped as soon as she saw Carly. She wasn't sure she could identify her, but she knew everything. She was torn up by Lamar's death. She saw it in her face. Hurt people hurt people. She knew that was Carly's intent. It was written all over her face. She took one more look around her living room. There was nothing there that couldn't be replaced. She put the letter in an envelope with his name written on the front and placed it on the mantelpiece. She grabbed her bag and left through the back entrance. She had heard that The Orient was wonderful this time a year. She looked forward to seeing Grayson Jeffcoat again, and she was certain he would be dying to see her.

Twenty

It was as if his truck had sprouted wings and flown to Jordan's house. He didn't see her car in the driveway, and the garage door was down. He got out of his truck, gun drawn. He knocked on the door. "Jordan," he said. "JORDAN!" He screamed at the top of his lungs. No one came to the door. He turned the doorknob, and it opened right up. He checked the living room area. There was no one. He looked towards the stairs, the bathroom, nothing. He saw an envelope with his name written on it, and he knew what he feared the most had happened. She was gone. He ripped open the envelope to find a letter that read,

"Dear Grayson,

If you are here reading this note, it means I'm gone. It also means that I had to run because you have undoubtedly found me out. I know that Carly gave you what information she could, and you put two and two together. You may even know about the evidence Victoria had, but I'm not sure. I will help you solve your cases. I killed David. He was a bastard and deserved everything I did to him. He had abused me, and I owed him. As for Lizzie, I had waited a lifetime to get her back. She was a vile creature. This was her payback for my mother, for Marcus, and even for James. I hope she rots a thousand years in the pit of hell. As for Lamar and Victoria, well, they were casualties of war. Victoria was too meddlesome, and you were right Grayson, she was a brilliant detective. I'm sure the force will miss her. As will you. I needed you to feel loss. I wanted you to feel what I feel every day, what I've felt for years. Lamar, on the other hand, was just in the wrong place at the wrong time. He had done everything I wanted him to, but that was my only opportunity to punish you and rid myself of your sidekick. I do have feelings. I've mourned Lamar every day since. So here you have it, Grayson. My confession. What are you going to do with it? Are you going to turn me in? Are you going to start an international manhunt for me? You know I have the means to hide anywhere. I'm good at it. I've spent an eternity being invisible. I don't think you will do it. You want to find me yourself. You know you do, and I'm not completely convinced it's because you want to turn me over to the authorities. Think about it. I'll be in touch. Love, Jordan."

Grayson couldn't believe it. She had confessed to all of it and dared him to turn her in. He looked down, and it was as if his feet were stuck in concrete. He couldn't decide what to do. He grabbed the envelope and ran out the door, only catching a glimpse of the handkerchief she had left on the end table—a perfect souvenir for her perfect crimes.

www.ingramcontent.com/pod-product-compliance
Lightning Source LLC
Chambersburg PA
CBHW071909200326

41519CB00016B/4549